I was edified by reading THINK ABOUT IT and found it theologically sound. Joan has created a wonderful work of reflection, meditation, and spiritual observation. I plan to purchase several copies to share with those who are seeking a richer faith life.

Fr. Sebastian Naslund, OSB, Valpariso, FL

The author's insight and spirituality makes this collection of thoughts an inspirational walk in faith, hope and joy wrapped in the goodness of God's love. Here are a few of my random comments on the essays: "A good guide for how to pray for others; excellent food for thought and action; her suggestions are invitingly simple and motivating; Joan has an incredible ability to simplify deep spiritual concerns for application into daily living; the essays are beautifully worded and filled with grace; she displays excellent coverage of each subject; and when I read "Voice of Love" I wept at the author's understanding in regard to God's love for souls.

Gloria Hart, The Villages, Fl

Joan Waller's faith is pure and deep. She is able to infuse her comments with a refreshing and unique insight, which has the net effect of having a universal appeal for any reader.

L. Mancini, Camp Hill, PA

Joan S. Waller

Think About It

Walking in the Fullness of Faith.
A Spiritual Perspective

Joan Sodaro Waller

WestBow
PRESS
A DIVISION OF THOMAS NELSON

ISBN: 978-1-4497-4362-8 (sc)
ISBN: 978-1-4497-4361-1 (e)
ISBN: 978-1-4497-4363-5 (hc)

Library of Congress Control Number: 2012904984

WestBow Press books may be ordered through booksellers or by contacting:

WestBow Press
A Division of Thomas Nelson
1663 Liberty Drive
Bloomington, IN 47403
www.westbowpress.com
1-(866) 928-1240

WestBow Press rev. date: 04/10/2012

For The Greater Glory Of God

To my grandparents, Giuseppe and Concetta Mangione Sodaro, and Ellen Horgan McIntosh, who passed along the Catholic Faith to my parents,

To my parents, Joseph and Margret McIntosh Sodaro, who brought me to know about and to receive the Sacraments of Baptism, Confirmation, Reconciliation, Eucharist, Marriage, and the Anointing of the Sick,

To my cousin, Mary Ann Koppes, who was my model in Faith,

To my brothers and sisters, Dean, Donald, Janet, and Margaret, who walked with me in Faith during our childhood and later years,

To my children, Margaret, Thomas, and James, whom we introduced into the life of Christ,

To my grandchildren Matthew, Christina, John, Robert, Alexa, and Taylor, who became children of God as infants,

To my husband, Bob, who facilitated me in the pursuit of my interest in obtaining a deeper understanding of my Faith through conferences, pilgrimages, lectures, prayer meetings, and daily Mass, and encouraged me to offer study groups in our home and to purchase all the literature I desired,

And last but not least, for all my companions who journeyed with me along the way to a more profound understanding of all the Catholic Church has to offer any person who desires to come into the fullness of the Christian Faith.

Preface

Essays On The Christian Life In Bits And Pieces

FOR CENTURIES, SAINTS AND scholars have probed the depths of the Catholic Faith—its beliefs, its practices, its history, and the experiences of those who lived its life to the fullest. They have written hundreds of billions of words in an effort to communicate the riches of the Catholic Faith to mankind. Unfortunately, few people have either the interest or the time to probe this vast body of inspiration. Most don't even know it exists.

Therefore, I offer bits and pieces of this wisdom. I offer it in a form that is easy to pick up and ponder. Think about one essay at a time, or perhaps one a day, so there's time to digest the underlying meaning. This method can benefit even the busiest person. Each article, each paragraph, and each sentence contains one bite of inspiration on which to chew. Pray over each thought and permit the wisdom, contained within, to penetrate and transform your life.

Carry these essays in the car. Place them on the nightstand. Keep a copy in the kitchen. Feed on it daily until it nourishes the spirit as food nourishes the body and knowledge nourishes the mind. By doing this, I guarantee that your daily faith life will be enriched and the fruits of the spirit—love, joy, peace, patience, kindness, longsuffering, faith, modesty, chastity, and reverence for God will blossom forth as you draw

CLOSER TO THE HEART OF CHRIST.

Contents

A Changed Perspective 1

Alive With Meaning 3

An Appointed Time 4

Benefits Of The Cross 5

Bodies Need Heads 7

Bruised Fruit 9

Called To Holiness 11

Choice: Blessing Or Curse 13

Commitment: It's Not A Dirty Word 15

Compatible Couple: The Church And The Sinner 17

Confirmation And The Holy Spirit 20

Take Time To Ponder #1 23

Contrary Mary 24

To Win 26

Conversion And Sanctification 27

Different Worlds 29

Establish A Serious Connection 31

Faith And Discipline 33

Faith-Building Reflections 37

Feeding On God's Word 39

Finding The Path To Truth And Unity 40

Fruitful Deeds 43

Take Time To Ponder #2 47

Getting Off Life's Teeter-Totter 48

Go Stand In The Gap 49

God Invites Us To Fulfillment 51

Has The Power Gone? 52

Spiritual Friendship 54
Hundredfold Return 56
I Love My Pet... 58
Invitation To The Quiet Life 59
Meditation On Pain 63
It's Like Planting A Garden 64
Joined Together In Christ 66
Journey Into Truth 68
Joy Of Submission... 70
Keys To Freedom 71
Take Time To Ponder #3 73
Like Conversation Prayer Flows........................ 74
"Londonderry Aire".. 76
Lord, Give Me Faith 78
Loving, Bearing, Sharing 79
Mini Reflection On Joy 80
New Life Unfolds Unobserved 81
O Lord, I Know You Are Near 83
On Being Hoodwinked 85
One Resolution: Two Approaches...................... 87
One Thing Leads To Another 89
Not A Victimless Crime 90
Praying Scripture A Key To Holiness 92
Private Litany For Humility 94
Take Time To Ponder #4 95
Reaching Out.. 96
Reluctant Samaritan 98
Scripture Meditations.................................... 100
Set Free! 102
Set The Record Straight 103
Sharing Our Treasures 104
Sing Praise.. 105
"Snack Pack" Of Thoughts 107
Statements And Questions 109
The Sacred Gift 112

Thirsting 114
To Acquire "It" 117
Take Time To Ponder #5 118
Treasure Rediscovered... 119
Universal Corruption 121
Unwanted? 123
Vulnerable?.. 124
We Fall On Our Faces 129
We're All In This Together 130
What Is Like A Filthy Garage?.............................. 131
Who Needs Them?.. 133
Who's In Charge? 135
Who's Speaking?... 137
Why Should Christians Pray? 139
With Joyful Hearts 141
Take Time To Ponder #6 143
Voice Of Love 144
Hungry For More? 148
Prayer To Release The Holy Spirit........................ 149

A Changed Perspective

KNOWING ABOUT JESUS AND knowing/loving Jesus as the power within are two different experiences. Since childhood, the Catholic Church has been the center of my life. The Church taught me about Jesus, and through the Church I found meaning, purpose, and direction. I relied on the Church to feed me the truth intellectually, to nourish me spiritually with the Sacraments, and to guide my moral life with the Wisdom of God. I found peace and security through obedience and faithfulness to the Church's teachings and guidance. For this I will be eternally grateful and blessed.

However, during the turbulent 1960s, membership in a Scripture study group moved my knowledge and love of Jesus and the Church from my head to my heart. Scripture challenged me to live and to proclaim Gospel values in a powerful way. The more I studied, the more my interest in worldly pursuits diminished. Soon countless projects in service of God, the Church, and the community filled my days. It proved to be a happy time full of meaningful activities, but I soon found myself exhausted and discouraged and my family neglected.

Somehow I had the mistaken idea that I needed to earn God's love, and, by my own power, to change myself and the world around me. But my struggle to change myself and to mend the world's ills proved too much. As a result, I suffered from overload and discouragement and noticed that nothing had changed for the better. Then God called a "time out." I'm grateful for the lessons I learned during those busy, exciting years and for all the fun I experienced working with my Catholic friends. But most of all I am grateful for the "time out."

The "time out" gave me time for prayer and study, which brought me to experience an encounter with the person of Jesus and the

1

release of the power of the Holy Spirit in my life. I had fallen madly and passionately in love with Jesus and with Mary, His blessed Mother. Now, in addition to what I had previously acquired, my perspective changed. I was on fire with love.

Slowly, expectant trust in God's transforming power replaced striving. Jesus replaced me and my ideas as the center of my existence. Prayer replaced anxiety, and knowing Jesus replaced just knowing about Him.

Hunger and openness are the keys that unlock the door of our souls to deeper conversion, to inner peace and power. When we let go and invite God to come dwell within us, and when we open our lives to the person and work of the Holy Spirit, we experience God's presence within us as He directs and guides us in His ways. Scripture teaches us that it is truly Jesus who works to accomplish His Will in us and through us.

Come closer and don't be afraid. Those who have followed the calling of God's Spirit and dug deeper into the Faith have caught the fire of Christ's love. We are all called to this deeper, richer relationship. All we have to do is say, Yes, I want more! But we must let go of preconceived notions and prejudices and fear. Even if one thinks he or she has it all, believe me, he or she doesn't. None of us has. There's an ocean of graces, knowledge, wisdom, inspiration, and the love of God just waiting for us to enjoy. Take, eat and enjoy!

Alive With Meaning

"I Believe" "Our Father" "Hail Mary"

THESE WORDS WHICH BEGIN the three most basic prayers of our Faith are packed with powerful material for reflection as are the words that follow. We (together) believe" or "I (alone) believe." What does it mean to believe? How does believing effect and reflect in the way I live? How does it change the meaning of my existence? Do I really believe, or am I just mouthing the words?

"Our Father" Notice the collective modifier. It means we together as a family; not just me. He's Our Father. What about father? What does the title "father" mean to me? What's my experience of father? Is that what God the Father is like, or is He quite different? How can I find out? Is He loving, forgiving, compassionate, and ready to help at all times? Is He constantly beside me and in me and in all of us? Or is He only a lawgiver, a judge, a jury, and an executioner? Which is the truth?

"Hail Mary" Who is she? Who hailed her and why? When I think about her, how does she come across? What is she really like? What role does she play in my life? What role should she play? Why was she chosen? What makes her different or special? How should I relate to her? What difference would it make?

Instead of racing through the words of these and other prayers, maybe we should pause after each word or two, think about them prayerfully, and ask the Holy Spirit for guidance. Perhaps then prayer would nourish our faith and draw us into a warmer and more loving relationship with God.

Even at Mass (the sacred liturgy), praying the prayers slowly and in a more thoughtful manner would surely draw us into unity with Christ.

An Appointed Time

"THERE'S AN APPOINTED TIME for everything and a time for every affair under the heavens."—Ecclesiastes 3:1.

There's a provident rhythm to life, and the origin of this rhythm is the Passion, Death, and Resurrection of Jesus Christ. In all joy and sorrow, we sing praise to God and accept all things in joy, for we know our lives are in the hands of our loving Father.

Everyone's life has a continual series of ups and downs. However, if we keep the paschal mystery of Jesus' Death and Resurrection in mind, we will recognize how our lives form a series of deaths and resurrections until we reach our final death and subsequent resurrection into eternal life.

No matter how difficult a burden we find ourselves bearing, we are assured that this burden will eventually pass over into liberation. As soon as we enter into a period of suffering and darkness (crucifixion), we can rejoice because we are already on our way to healing and wholeness (resurrection).

Jesus is our sign of hope. So we too need to be a sign of hope to others since we live in Jesus, and He is continually dying and rising in us. Staying united to Jesus and "gambling on" Him guarantees us the joyous victory of resurrection both now and for all eternity.

Benefits Of The Cross

On December 2, 1899, Jesus asked Servant of God Luisa Piccarreta to tell Him "what the cross is and what the cross does." She used the following phrases to describe The Cross:

- "Fruitful and is that which gives birth to grace."
- "Light."
- "Fire and reduces to ashes all that is not of God."
- "A coin of inestimable value."
- "The coin that is gained by suffering on Earth and is the money that circulates in Heaven."
- "That which gives me knowledge of myself and knowledge of God."
- "That which grafts me into the virtues."
- "The seat of uncreated Wisdom and teaches me the most high doctrines, subtle, and sublime."
- "The way God unveils to me the most secret mysteries, the most hidden things, and the most perfection which is hidden to the most learned and wise of the world."
- "The water that not only purifies me but provides the nourishment for the virtues to grow in me."
- "The celestial dew that preserves and beautifies in me the beautiful lily of purity."
- "The food of hope."
- "The torch of working Faith."
- "That which always preserves, maintains and enkindles the fire of Charity."
- "That dry wood that makes vanish and puts to flight all the smoke of pride and vainglory and produces the humble violet of humility."

- "That most powerful arm that assails the devils and defends me from all their clutches."
- "Is the envy and admiration of the Angels and Saints and the rage and anger of the devils."
- "My paradise on earth."
- "The chain of gold that connects me with God in the most intimate union."
- "That which makes my being disappear and transmutes me into you, my God, my Beloved object."
- "That which makes me feel lost in God and makes me able to live on His very Life."

Jesus affirmed Luisa's description and said, "Bravo, bravo, my beloved. You have spoken well." He added, "**The cross is so powerful; and I have communicated to it so much Grace as to render it more efficacious than the Sacraments themselves ... because the cross has the power to dispose the soul to Grace.**"

Unpublished vol. 3, pages 12-13 BOOK OF HEAVEN by Luisa Piccarreta

Bodies Need Heads

WHAT HAPPENS TO A body without a head, a ship without a rudder, sheep without a shepherd, or people without an authority outside themselves or a rule to guide them?

Isn't that the way life is lived today? Each person tries to function on his or her own. They make up their own rules and do whatever they please without concern for others or for what pleases God. No one is in control. Everyone is a law unto himself or herself. Like chickens without heads running and grasping at anything or anyone to fill their emptiness.

The human race needs someone in authority. The human race needs to be obedient to someone and something outside itself. Children do, and pets do, and adults surely do too.

When God created the human race He endowed us with free will so we could be like Him—free to choose. Even after Adam and Eve sinned, God left us with this priceless gift. But now, because of original sin, we are in a weakened state.

St. Paul complained: **"What I do, I do not understand. For I do not do what I want, but I do what I hate"**—Romans 7:15. **"For I know that good does not dwell in me, that is, in my flesh. The willing is ready at hand, but doing the good is not"**—Romans 7:18.

Paul also speaks about authority: **"Let every person be subordinate to the higher authorities, for there is no authority except from God, and those that exist have been established by God. Therefore, whoever resists authority opposes what God has appointed, and those who oppose it will bring judgment upon themselves"**—Romans 13:1–2.

Jesus knew that truth about us, His creations. He knew how rebellious we would be once we stopped living in the Divine Will and how we would let our human wills reign over us with all our passions on fire. "But you, beloved, remember the words spoken beforehand by the apostles of our Lord Jesus Christ, for they told you, 'In [the] last time there will be scoffers who will live according to their own godless desires. These are the ones who cause divisions; they live on the natural plane, devoid of the Spirit'"—Jude 1:17–19.

Jesus knew how much we needed grace and guidance and authority. That's why He established His church and gave it the authority to teach, to govern, and to sanctify us. "He said to Peter: 'And so I say to you, you are Peter, and upon this rock I will build my church and the gates of the netherworld shall not prevail against it. I will give to you the keys to the kingdom of heaven. Whatever you bind on earth shall be bound in heaven. Whatever you loose on earth shall be loosed in heaven'"—Matthew 16:18–19. Thus, Peter was given authority to be the first to guide the Church, the Mystical Body of Christ, after Christ's resurrection.

"Then Jesus approached and said to [the disciples], 'All power in heaven and on earth has been given to me. Go, therefore, and make disciples of all nations, baptizing them in the name of the Father, and of the Son, and of the Holy Spirit, teaching them to observe all that I commanded you. And behold I am with you always, until the end of the age'"—Matthew 28: 18–20.

For two thousand years the same pattern has been followed. Obedience to this authority is the necessary principle for unity, peace, holiness, and love. Without obedience, the Body of Christ becomes fractured. The Church needs an authentic head in order for the Body to function as Christ desires. And each of us must use our free will to choose the right path.

"Jesus said to [Thomas]: 'I am the way and the truth and the life. No one comes to the Father except through me'"—John 14:6. Jesus also said, "I am the light of the world; whoever follows me will not walk in darkness, but will have the light of life"—John 8:12. "Jesus then said to the Jews who believed in him, 'If you remain in my word, you will truly be my disciples, and you will know the truth, and the truth will set you free'"—John 8:31–32.

Jesus knows that bodies need heads, and so does the Church.

Bruised Fruit

HAVE YOU EVER FOUND that the fruits of the Spirit that are most easily bruised are the fruits of peace, love, and joy? Have you ever been going along just as happily as possible when suddenly something or someone gets under your skin? Some irritating thought, some irritating person, or some irritating situation bumps against you and bruises your peace, love, and joy? I don't know about you, but it certainly happens to me.

I finally grew tired of these delightful fruits getting bruised, so I decided to analyze the underlying conditions that make these fruits in my life so vulnerable. I thought about what I could do to change these conditions and how I might counteract the bruising bumps.

First, I recognized how my perfectionist compulsion opens me to many irritations. Having perfectionist leanings doesn't mean I do everything perfectly. It only means I'd like everything and everyone, including me, to be beautiful, wholesome, law abiding holy, neat and orderly. Unfortunately, only God meets this desire.

Second, because I am a sensate person I am sensitive to everything around me. My sense of sight, sound, taste, smell, order, beauty, and touch keep me constantly aware of all things. This is both a blessing and a curse.

Third, in the moral and spiritual realm I am sensitive to goodness as well as to sin and error in all their forms. Preaching and teaching words spew forth and condemning thoughts follow. These in turn deal the final blow. Now the fruits of peace, love, and joy are not only bruised, they are rotten.

Therefore, to preserve peace, love, and joy on a moment-to-moment basis I decided to implement the following techniques that indeed help preserve those wonderful fruits.

- Recognize the irritation as a temptation to become angry, judgmental, and hateful.
- Pray for help, wisdom, and the power to act against the irritation.
- Refuse to allow the irritation to overwhelm me. Run away from the person or the situation if I can't keep your mouth closed. If I can't flee, then close my mouth very tightly.
- Stand firm against the irritation and rebuke it in Jesus' name.
- To counterattack, replace the irritating thought with a loving thought; listen with an open heart and an open mind.
- Speak the truth as I understand it and let that seed of truth take root.
- If possible, act to correct the person's "flaw," but only if I can do it with love.
- Let God and time deal with the person or the situation.
- Continue to pray that God's Will prevails in that person's life and in mine.
- Remember, I can't change others. I can only change myself with God's grace.
- Most important! Praise God in all situations. "We know that all things work for good for those who love God, who are called according to his purpose"—Romans 8:28.

Like you, I don't care for bruised fruit, for slivers under my skin, or for burrs under my saddle, but I do care for peace, love, and joy. Thus far, this battle plan has definitely helped to preserve these desirable fruits of the Holy Spirit. Thank you, Father.

Called To Holiness

FORGIVENESS, TRUST, AND OPENNESS to Grace are keys to freedom and growth. When we forgive and trust, we are free to love. "God is love." So when we love, we are in God.

Paul tells us that God "**chose us in him [Christ], before the foundation of the world, to be holy and without blemish before him**"—Ephesians 1:4. That's what a truly genuine and wholesome human being should be like. Let's not run away from God. Instead, let's run toward Him if we desire to become holy, blameless, and full of love. Let's yield each area of our lives to His power and His grace.

Jesus told **us "I am the vine, you are the branches. Whoever remains in me and I in him will bear much fruit, because without me you can do nothing**"—John 15:5. Striving to achieve holiness through our own efforts brings about pride and self-righteousness, which is the opposite of holiness. Rather, holiness comes about through the power of God working through those who believe and who cooperate with His grace.

First we accept God's unconditional love for us. Then we ask Him to help us love ourselves and others unconditionally, never allowing us to look down on ourselves or others. Remember, God doesn't make mistakes, nor does He produce junk. Each of us is loved by God no matter how sinful or imperfect we may be. He loves us, warts and all.

Loving oneself is not conceit. Instead, it's an act that opens the door to grace and gives us the ability to love God, ourselves, and others. It also opens the door to forgiveness and trust, which make holiness possible. The mistakes we make as we walk with God toward holiness can be opportunities for growth. "**Accept the things that cannot change, ask for courage to change the things that can,**

and pray for wisdom to know the difference"—Serenity Prayer by theologian Reinhold Niebuhr..

Sing praise to God for everything that happens, for nothing can happen to us without God's permission. He will use each occasion to bring about growth to those who are open to the grace of the present moment. Challenge opens new channels of His Grace. Never despair, never give up! Trust in God! Forgive yourself and others! Accept the challenges and watch the miracle of growth take place within.!

God always loves us no matter how much we have sinned. Scripture says that nothing can separate us from His love. It isn't God who chooses where we spend eternity, in spite of what most of us have heard. St. Catherine of Genoa came to realize that when we come face-to-face with God at the time of our death, we will see the truth about our condition and realize that we are not worthy to stand before Him. Then we will literally throw ourselves into Purgatory to be cleansed or into Hell to suffer forever. Jesus came to save us. Our response calls for a wholehearted return of love, repentance, acceptance of the gift of forgiveness, belief in Him, and obedience to His Divine and Holy Will.

Choice: Blessing Or Curse

FREEDOM OF CHOICE (FREE will) is a gift from God, our wise and loving Father. His commandments are also His gift. So it isn't a question of whether we have freedom of choice but rather a question of how wisely we choose. Scripture tells us, **"I set before you here, this day, a blessing or a curse: a blessing for obeying the commandments of the Lord, your God … a curse if you do not obey the commandments of the Lord, your God, but turn aside from the way I ordain for you today, to follow other gods"**— Deuteronomy 11:26–28).

Compare two images of God. Which do we choose?

Choose a permissive God who says, "If it feels good, do it"? Ask your friends. If they say it's okay, then it must be. Follow the crowd. Do what everyone else does without asking God for advice. Unfortunately, the "god of feelings" and the "god of subjectivity" are the gods that most people choose to follow.

Those whose lives are guided by the permissive God lead lives cursed by misguided decisions, the natural consequence of which are broken and unfulfilled lives and the loss of eternal life. Consider the natural consequence of the use of illicit drugs and overconsumption of nicotine or alcohol. Consider the results of a lifestyle where power, money, possessions, and illicit sex are the center of interest, or a lifestyle of overindulgence in anything. The list is endless. Where do they lead? They lead to ill health, broken relationships, broken hearts, and loss of eternal life.

Anytime we choose anything but God's Will, we lose the very freedom we covet. We fall under the power of sin, evil, Satan, and addiction. We become weakened, sick, helpless, and out of control. We open ourselves to misery, death, and chaos.

Unfortunately, we live in a world where freedom from rules, laws, and regulations are said to be the height of freedom, but instead, that kind of license can lead to anarchy.re said to be the height of freedom, but instead, that kind of license can lead to anarchy.

Choose an authoritative God who we believe knows what is best for us and who has and does communicate His Will? Those whose lives are guided by the authoritative God receive the blessings of joy, peace, and fulfillment now and eternal happiness after death. Consider the natural consequences of a well ordered life of discipline, obedience, faithfulness, hard work, generosity, thoughtfulness, faith, hope, and above all, self-sacrificial love of God, self, and others. Actually, the only people who don't need rules, laws, and regulations are people who love, who are disciplined, and who have God as their source of strength, goodness, and freedom.

Church laws and society's laws are meant to protect us and lead us to well ordered, disciplined, and fulfilled lives. Rather than bondage, they are paths to freedom and joy. It's not the rules, laws, and regulations themselves that make us holy, happy, and free people. It's the power of God working within us when we follow them.

Jesus came that we might have life and have it more abundantly. That's His promise and His desire. Anyone who wants to be freed from destructive behavior can be set free. Sincere repentance and calling on the power of God in the Name of Jesus, especially through the Sacrament of Penance, pours out powerful graces upon us.

Being forgiven is easy. That's why Jesus, the Son of God, became man. However, remaining free takes our cooperation. Discard seductive friends, join a healthy Catholic community, receive the Sacraments often, find a mature and prayerful Catholic friend to help you, read Scripture often, and pray for guidance, strength, and wisdom.

Rules aren't hoops to jump through but rather guides to true peace. Cooperating and relying on God's grace empowers us both to desire and to follow His Will without having to struggle. Wise choices lead to true freedom as well as to abundant life and the blessings of peace, joy, and true love.

Commitment: It's Not A Dirty Word

TODAY IT SEEMS THAT commitment is a dirty word to a world where choice and leaving options open is the "in thing." Generally speaking, in the past, employer and employee exhibited a deep sense of love and commitment to their work, to their community, and to each other.

Loyalty and self-sacrifice also went hand-in-hand with deep commitment to Jesus and the Church. A sense of unity and concern for one another permeated the atmosphere, like a family or a team pulling together toward a common goal. The words "committed," "loyal," "hardworking," and "self-sacrificing" would describe most people.

Nowadays, one would be hard-pressed to find this kind of situation. Commitment is out. Instead, self-centeredness, individuality, strife, division, competition, disorder, and an attitude of "let's keep our options open" permeate our lives. "Looking out for number one" is the norm. Commitment to church, family, and God's commandments has been pushed aside, where they wither and die for lack of interest.

Lack of commitment to God and self-centeredness lead to a lack of commitment on the job, in the home, in the community, and between individuals. Without commitment to Christ, the foundation for commitment to anything or to anyone erodes. Whereas, commitment to Christ fuels commitment to the good of others rather than commitment to self-centered concerns.

To commit oneself means to speak or act in such a manner as to bind oneself to a certain line of conduct, to confidently put oneself into the care of another one trusts.

If I'm not committed to Jesus, then to whom or what am I committed. When that person, belief, or object fails to live up to my expectations, I lose faith and separate myself from that person, idea, or object. Then I either commit myself to another or I strike out on my own. If I trust in no one but myself and then fail to live up to my own expectations, I may become clinically depressed, or else I might strike out and blame other people or circumstances for my distress. The person might be thinking, since everyone and everything interferes with my peace, I must search for a better and more trustful relationship.

Thus the cycle begins again. Each time this happens, broken dreams, broken lives, broken homes, abandoned jobs, and diluted principles result. Dissatisfaction, emptiness, striving, striking back, loneliness, discouragement, and anger drive me away from others and others are driven away from me. The hollowness of my life betrays me as I grasp for any means to satisfy my insatiable hungers and unbridled passions.

Not so for one who has cultivated a commitment to Jesus. Jesus never fails to live up to my expectations. If I follow His way of love, I'll never find myself disappointed. Jesus' way of love bears all things, believes all things, and hopes all things. This kind of love teaches me to put others first and to sacrifice myself on behalf of another. It opens me to the truth about myself so I begin to see myself as I really am. It teaches me to walk in the way of justice and mercy. It gives me strength to forgive, to forget, and to love in spite of being hurt.

Commitment to Jesus and to His Way builds community because it teaches everyone to look to the needs of others rather than to their own and to work untiringly for the common good. Commitment to Jesus breeds compassion, understanding, and self-sacrifice. It builds up rather than tears down.

What a wonderful world this would be if commitment to Jesus and obedience to His Way became the foundation of every society, looking to the interests of others rather than to one's own. No, commitment is not a dirty word but a word filled with promise for all.

Compatible Couple: The Church And The Sinner

Two BASIC PRINCIPLES NEED to be recognized before we can discuss the subject of the compatible couple: the Church and the sinner.

The Church: The Mystical Body of Christ was established by Jesus to rescue all sinners and to reconcile us to the Father through the Holy Spirit working through the Sacraments.

The sinner: The Original Sin of Adam and Eve destroyed our intimate relationship with God. Because of this, our human will is weakened, and we find it difficult to be obedient.

The Church begins to rescue the sinner through the Sacrament of Baptism which destroys Original Sin. Then the Church strengthens the weakened human will by feeding the soul with grace through the other six Sacraments. For instance, Confirmation strengthens us for the battle against the three sources of sin: the temptations of the world, the flesh, and the devil. It feeds us the Holy Eucharist (the Bread of Life and the Cup of Eternal Salvation) to nourish us along the way. It forgives our sins and cleanses us through the Sacraments of Reconciliation (Penance) and the Anointing Of The Sick. Then, it pours out special graces to aid us in our vocations of Matrimony and Holy Orders.

Through the centuries Christ's Church has provided a roadmap by teaching and interpreting God's Ten Commandments (the moral law) for us. It sets down disciplinary laws for us to follow. These help us grow in virtue as we seek to be obedient to God who speaks to us through the One, Holy, Catholic, and Apostolic Church as we follow Jesus each moment of our lives. The Church and the Sinner are bound together in mutual harmony. They are completely compatible. The one cannot live without the other. Jesus said to Peter, **"you are**

Peter, and upon this rock I will build my church, and the gates of the netherworld shall not prevail against it"—Matthew 16:18. He died for each of us and established the Church. He commissioned it to teach, to govern, and to sanctify us because he knew our weakness and our sinfulness.

Jesus' greatest desire is to forgive every person, to set them free, and to fill them with His very own Life. The Church is there to help us reach that goal as we submit to her authority and are graced by her blessings. It is not there to condemn us!

Commitment to Christ and a sincere desire to please him are the foundations of a holy life. When we fail, we feel guilty and seek forgiveness in the Sacrament of Penance (Reconciliation). If certain sins have become embedded in us, we need to seek out counseling and spiritual direction to help us get to the bottom and source of the problem. To become a Saint we must come to know the moral laws set down by the Ten Commandments, which the Church interprets for us and for our benefit. Then as we follow this guidance by the power of God's grace, praying constantly for help, God will fill our souls with new life and we will be at peace.

All the ideals and the commandments of the Catholic Faith are difficult, and many times we will fail to measure up. Guilty feelings help brings us into the reality of our state before God. He knows how difficult it is to live a holy life because we are so weakened by Original Sin. But we must reach up to the ideal, to do our best, and to desire always to do what pleases God who speaks to us through His Church.

It is childish to continually blame the institution of the Church for calling us to a perfection we constantly fail to achieve. Sacrifice is basic to our Faith. Sacrifice means to deny ourselves all kinds of illicit pleasures. This in turn leads us to sanctity.

Satisfying our passions leads us into grave physical, moral, and spiritual danger and kills God's life within us. The "road" that is wide leads us to destruction, and that is the world's way. Therefore, choose the narrow "road." Stay away from temptation! **Keeping away from the circumstances or the people who lead us into sin is**

absolutely required. Because God loves us without reserve, He will forgive us as often as and as long as we are sorry.

All He asks of us is to believe in Him, to trust Him, and to obey Him. But most of all, He yearns to have us love Him unconditionally just as He loves us Sinners. God cannot work effectively in our lives unless these conditions are met.

When we start on a trip, we know that we need a roadmap or a GPS. Otherwise we can expect to make wrong turns and end up lost, never reaching our destination. It is the same with life. If we don't have a map, a guidebook, or an intelligent voice to guide us as we travel through life, how can we expect to make the right choices? How can we expect to reach the goal of Heaven and enjoy eternal happiness with God?

Jesus calls us to repent and to believe the Good News. Jesus has come to save everyone in the whole world. He left us the Catholic Church to guide us. We have feet of clay and are going to continue to fail and not live up to Christ's way without the guidance, the teaching, and the sanctifying Church. Desiring to do what is right, living up to the ideal, and repenting when we fail will help us reach our destination. Thanks be to God, we Sinners are blessed with the Church, a sure roadmap or a GPS to Heaven.

Confirmation And The Holy Spirit

IN GOD'S VIEW, JUST how does the Sacrament of Confirmation fit into the life of a Christian? Have we sold this Sacrament short? Should it be considered simply a social Sacrament that makes us adult members of the church, or should Confirmation be expected to have similar effects on the life of every baptized person as Scripture says it did on the first Disciples?

Jesus instructed them **"to wait for 'the promise of the Father about which you have heard me speak; for John baptized with water, but in a few days you will be baptized with the holy Spirit'"**—Acts 1:4–5; and **"'you will receive power when the holy Spirit comes upon you, and you will be my witnesses in Jerusalem, throughout Judea and Samaria, and to the ends of the earth'"**—Acts 1:8. Read on in Acts to see what happened to them as a result.

Those who have sincerely asked for the release of the Spirit, given to us in Baptism and Confirmation, now find they are eager to speak about Jesus and to witness to his power and presence in their lives whenever the opportunity presents itself. The Holy Spirit empowers a person with a spirit of boldness which makes them eager to share the Good News of Jesus with others and to be actively engaged in God's work.

Through Confirmation we became soldiers of Christ, and as a result, our lives should reflect a dynamic relationship and love affair between ourselves and God making us eager to tell others how Jesus and His life-giving Spirit have made us mature members of His Body. Through Baptism and Confirmation we received the Holy Spirit, so why does it take us years to finally allow the Spirit's presence and power to become visible in our words and actions? Why for so long do our lips remain sealed, and the ability to witness to God's redeeming love remain dormant?

To this day, many committed clergy, religious and laypeople are unable to speak freely about Jesus or are unwilling to speak about their Faith openly and joyfully without embarrassment. Why do we hold back? What's keeping our lips locked?

Perhaps the fault lies in the way Confirmation is presented. Or perhaps the fault lies in the fact that so many of our teachers and preachers are not "on fire" with the Holy Spirit. Instead they impart only theological information about the Holy Spirit rather than share firsthand knowledge.

To create the desire to open oneself and to unlock the reality of the Spirit's power, one must come to know and expect this reality. If the emphasis of our preparation for Confirmation were to be placed on expectation, openness, and the desire to let go and let God's Spirit fill us with His love, His presence, and His power, then the doors of our hearts and minds would be awakened to receive this empowering impacted our lives, and we would be able to see the Spirit actively engaged in our lives.

What is needed is concrete teaching in regard to how the Spirit can empower us to turn away from our sinful habits; how the Spirit can heal and deliver us from sickness and evil; and how the Spirit can give us courage and wisdom to speak about and to live the Good News. Only when teachers, parents, clergy, and religious are filled with the dynamic life of the Holy Spirit will the Sacrament of Confirmation be able to enliven the rest of Body of Christ and the world. Like the Apostles after Pentecost, we would be able to set the world on fire with the Spirit's power. Remember though, one cannot give what one does not have.

God the Father anointed Jesus with the Spirit and power. Jesus breathed the Spirit on the Apostles, and in turn the Apostles, led by the Spirit, established the Church, and God empowered the Church to breathe the Spirit's life into a dying world. But this cannot be done by dead and dying Christians.

If we find that we can't or don't talk about Jesus, the Good News, or any aspect of our Faith with enthusiasm, conviction, and love, maybe it's time to invite the Holy Spirit to take over our lives and empower us. Invite Him to set us on fire with love for Jesus and loosen our tongues so we can proclaim to this dying world that "Jesus Christ is Lord!!!"

Let's stop being "do it myself" Christians. Instead, let's allow Jesus' Spirit to make us powerfully "alive in Christ."

Take Time To Ponder #1

IT'S MOST BENEFICIAL IF your reflections are written down and pondered often.

- Deep down inside, how much faith and trust do I have in God's loving providence? Can I say, "Father I put my life in your hands" and really mean it?
- Do I pray regularly for an increase of faith for myself?
- Do I have an attitude of "give me" when it comes to prayer, seeing God there only to answer my every whim?
- What is the purpose of prayer?
- Do I spend all my prayer time asking, or do I spend at least an equal amount of time giving thanks, expressing my love, and singing praise for all the blessings and challenges that God has allowed to come my way?
- Am I honest with God and with myself? Do I understand what I really want and why I want it?
- When I pray do I speak honestly about my feelings, or do I sugarcoat them?
- In my relationship with God, how important is praise?
- Do I pray to change God's mind or to open myself to His Will and His grace?
- Am I praying with a humble, submissive heart, or am I praying with a demanding, complaining, and proud heart?

Remember, faith and hope mean believing without seeing. Hope is no longer hope when the object is seen. Religious faith is an act of trust in someone—Jesus.

Contrary Mary

Mary, Mary quite contrary
How does your garden grow?
With silver bells and cockleshells
And pretty maids all in a row.

Poor Contrary Mary, she could only produce silver bells, cockleshells, and pretty maids instead of mature fruit in her garden.

Was that due to her contrariness?

What does "contrary" mean?

Am I contrary?

Are you contrary?

Contrary means behaving in an opposite manner: inclined to oppose or resist, to be antagonistic, to contradict, and to be perverse or adverse.

What made Mary contrary? To what was she opposed?

Since Contrary Mary is only a figment of some poet's imagination, let's look instead at ourselves and the spiritual gardens of our own souls.

How are we opposed, perverse, or adverse?

What causes our spiritual gardens to produce only "silver bells, cockleshells, and pretty maids" instead of loving, caring, holy, and virtuous lives.

What are God's rules for producing a fruit-filled spiritual garden in our souls?

He says to repent and to believe the Good News. Do we?

He says to obey His commandments. Do we?

He says to forgive those who wrong us and to forget those hurts. Do we?

He says to fast in some way or another. Do we?

He says to pray expectantly and always. Do we?

He says to rejoice in all things. Do we?

He says if we trust Him, He promises that all things will work together for our benefit. Do we?

He says to turn the other cheek. Do we?

He says to deny ourselves, take up our crosses without complaining. Do we?

He says to love our enemies and do good to those who harm us. Do we?

He says to come to Him when we are burdened. Do we?

He says to accept Jesus as our Lord and Savior and stop trying to save ourselves. Do we?

He says to let go and let Him be in control. Do we?

He says to eat the Bread of Life and to Drink the Cup of Salvation, the Eucharist. Do we?

He says we're not to be afraid. Are we?

Then, along with His "rule," He promises to give us all the help we need in order to obey and to act on His "rule."

Jesus, our Master Gardener asks us to yield every aspect of our lives to Him one by one—to let go and let Him be in charge so He can transform us.

WHAT AN INCREDIBLE OFFER! SO …

Why are we so contrary? Why do we oppose Him? Why do resist His call? Why do we insist on doing everything our way, by ourselves, when doing everything His way satisfies our hunger for happiness and produces a fruit-filled life?

The answer is very simple. We're proud, and our weak human wills constantly work against us. Therefore, if we don't ask for God's grace to help us we are doomed to failure.

Why not taste and see how good the Lord is and experience His merciful love. It's a free gift. Every day God eagerly waits for us to call out to Him so He can bestow upon us an abundant life of holiness and a garden of virtues in our souls. Let's do it

To Win

To get the best of the devil
Don't leave the door open
to negative thoughts.
Instead, keep your mind occupied
with thoughts of God
and concentrate on the work
He has given you to do,
singing praise with every breath.

Conversion And Sanctification

In Philippians 3:10 Paul says that we should "know [Christ] and the power of his resurrection and [the] sharing of his sufferings by being conformed to his death…" This is a good definition of the experience of falling in love with Jesus and being empowered by the Spirit to do God's work.

Be humble and rely solely on God, and you will be blessed.

Repent and believe in the Gospel, the message of joy. Let your repentance be filled with joy, not sorrow. Don't cling to the past. Move forward with hope, knowing your sins are forgiven.

Forgiveness is God's gift to us because He loves us. You do not have to earn His love through your own effort. Just accept it as a given.

The whole Christian community is involved in the reconciliation and the spiritual growth of individuals. We need to pray for each other for daily conversion and repentance.

A real conversion turns us away from ourselves and toward Jesus and others.

Our human relationships should always be guided by our love of the Lord Jesus, ourselves, and others.

Jesus became man to come close to us. Don't be afraid to come close to Him and to feel at home in His presence.

The signs of Salvation are as follows:

Effective progress toward a deeper more intimate relationship with the Blessed Trinity

An increasing manifestation of the fruits of the Holy Spirit in our lives: charity, joy, peace, patience, benignity, long suffering, faith, modesty, chastity, and fear of the Lord (awe and reverence toward God and His works)

Serenity and certainty of God's love and forgiveness
Purity of life
Missionary endeavor

Different Worlds

The worldly person
- Sees no need for God,
- Hungers for a culture of abundance,
- Insists that morality is an individual decision,
- Desires to live independently of others and do things his way,
- Is disinterested in building community,
- Lives a self-centered lifestyle,
- Insists that all that is unknown is discoverable,
- Finds mystery unacceptable,
- Analyzes everything scientifically,
- Forgets the past and denies judgment and eternal life,
- Constantly seeks new experiences to fill life's void,
- Expresses little or no commitment to anyone or anything,
- Sees multiple partners as desirable,
- Allows the science lab and the hospital to play God,
- Finds everything boring and dull,
- Has no time for dreams or hope, and,
- Denies the validity of a spiritual view of life.

The true Christian
- Recognizes his total dependence on God;
- Possesses a sense of mission;
- Is other-centered and outer directed;
- Flees concern for and is drawn to community;
- Accepts mystery as valid;
- Recognizes the past as valid;
- Lives in the present but keeps an eye on eternal life;

- Remembers and cherishes each experience;
- Enjoys commitment to persons, ideals, beliefs, values, etc.;
- Sees poetry, meaning, and value in all life;
- Knows there is more to life than can be seen or understood;
- Is blessed with deep insights into the realm of the spiritual world.

In which world do I stand?

Establish A Serious Connection

To build a serious relationship with God, it's important to establish a strong commitment to prayer.

- Start with ten or more minutes and regularly increase the time.
- Abandonment of self to God is crucial. Give Jesus all worries, fears, anxieties, and concerns.
- Then, with eyes closed, repeat the name of Jesus over and over while concentrating on His presence, using our imaginations.
- Another option is to repeat the entire Jesus Prayer: "Jesus Christ, Son of the living God, have mercy on me a sinner" until peace comes.
- Or just allow the Holy Spirit to pray with our spirit by using the gift of tongues.
- The Jesus Prayer and praying in the Spirit provides a protective shield over us. It sanctifies all that is in and around us. It strengthens all the gifts the Holy Spirit has bestowed on us and helps us become more effective disciples. It also brings about healing. Now we are ready to listen as God speaks to us.
- To grow in a serious relationship with God takes the discipline of prime time spent in daily prayer, which includes abandonment, Scripture reading, other spiritual reading, and various forms of prayer and silence.
- In order to really believe in Heaven, God wants us see and experience the healing and sanctifying power of

God in this life, as a foretaste of the eternal life in Heaven after death.

- Draw closer to Christ and reap the benefits now!
- Don't be afraid and don't wait!
- Jesus waits with open arms!

Faith And Discipline

"For in fire gold is tested and worthy men in
the crucible of humiliation"—Sirach 2:5.

Trials And Tribulations

OH HOW WE DREAD them. We worry about what did happen, what
is happening, and what may happen. We fear the future when we
consider all the possibilities that we may be called on to face.

We don't always see our prayers answered and we ask why. We
tend to doubt God's goodness and His trustworthiness.

We are tempted to question God's omnipotence or saving will
as the Israelites did so often.

The Old Testament is filled with examples of man tempting
God; that is, putting God to the test. Even His chosen people
questioned His Wisdom.

At one point after the Exodus the Israelites threaten to revolt
and return to Egypt, but Moses interceded for them with God. By
this time they had put God to the test ten times, and in spite of His
promise to forgive them, he declared that those who failed to trust
and failed to heed His voice would not be allowed to enter into the
Promised Land.

God says, "**Do not harden your hearts as at Meribah, as on
the day of Massah in the desert. There your ancestors tested me;
they tried me though they had seen my works**"—Psalm 95:8–9.
"**You shall not put the Lord your God to the test**"—Deuteronomy
6:16.

"**Let us not test Christ as some of them did, and suffered death
by serpents. Do not grumble as some of them did, and suffered
death by the destroyer**"—I Corinthians 10:9–10.

It sounds like God is not too pleased with us when we question His Wisdom and lose confidence in His ability to care of us.

"Faith is the realization of what is hoped for and evidence of things not seen"—Hebrews 11:1. "But without faith it is impossible to please him, for anyone who approaches God must believe that he exists and that he rewards those who seek him"—Hebrews 11:6.

Abraham "thought that the One who had made the promise was trustworthy"—Hebrews 11:11. "All these [Abel, Enoch, Noah, Abraham, and Sarah] died in faith. They did not receive what had been promised but saw it and greeted it from afar"—Hebrews 11:13. "Yet all these, though approved because of their faith, did not receive what had been promised"—Hebrews 11:39. (See footnote in Scripture for Hebrews 11:39.) The heroes of the Old Testament obtained their recompense only after the saving work of Christ had been accomplished. Thus they already enjoyed what Christians who are still struggling do not yet possess in its fullness.

Hebrews 11:1–40 tells what these ancient faithful people did:

ABEL offered a sacrifice greater than Cain's.

ENOCH was taken away without dying.

NOAH revered God and built an ark so that his household might be saved.

ABRAHAM went forth to the place he was to receive as a heritage not knowing where he was going. When put to the test, he offered up his son Isaac.

SARAH received the power to conceive though she was well past the age.

ISAAC invoked for Jacob and Esau blessings that were still to be.

JACOB blessed each of the sons of Joseph.

JOSEPH spoke of the exodus of the Israelites.

MOSES' parents hid him for three months, disregarding the king's edict.

MOSES refused to be known as the son of pharaoh's daughter. By faith he left Egypt, not fearing the king's wrath. He kept the Passover.

THE ISRAELITES crossed the Red Sea, and because of Israel's faith the walls of Jericho fell after being encircled.

By faith RAHAB escaped from being destroyed with the unbelievers, for she had peacefully received the spies.

GIDEON, BARAK, SAMSON, JEPHTHAH, DAVID, and SAMUEL and the PROPHETS by faith conquered kingdoms, did what was just, broke the jaws of lions, put out raging fires, escaped the devouring sword, and turned back foreign invaders.

STILL OTHERS endured mockery, scourging, even chains and imprisonment. They were stoned, sawed in two, put to death by sword. They went about garbed in the skins of sheep and goats, needy, afflicted, and tormented. They wandered about in deserts and on mountains. They dwelt in caves and in holes in the earth. Yet despite the fact that all of these were approved because of their faith, they did not obtain what had been promised. They held out to the end in spite of not obtaining the promise.

Good Advice

In Hebrews 12, Paul goes on to instruct and to encourage us in our faith walk.

- Get rid of sin. It encumbers and slowly destroys us.
- Persevere through thick and thin.
- Keep our eyes on Jesus, remembering how he endured the opposition of sinners.
- Don't grow despondent.
- Don't abandon the struggle.
- Endure all trials as the discipline of God, who deals with us as sons.

God's Discipline

"**My son, do not disdain the discipline of the Lord or lose heart when reproved by him; for whom the Lord loves, he disciplines; he scourges every son he acknowledges**"—Hebrews 12:5–6.

Paul talks about how we discipline our children to prepare them for the short span of mortal life. If a parent fails to discipline a child it is looked on as a disgrace. "**All discipline seems a cause not for joy** but for pain, yet later it brings the peaceful fruit of righteousness to those who are trained by it"—Hebrew 12:11.

"Besides this, we have had our earthly fathers to discipline us ... for a short time ... but [God] does so for our benefit, in order that we may share his holiness"—Hebrews 12:9–10). Therefore, we should regard our own sufferings as the affectionate correction of the Lord, who loves us as a father loves his children.

Let's heed God's warning to stop griping and complaining, questioning, and putting Him to the test. Instead, let's start praying for humility, patience, and an increase of faith and to trust His providence because Our Father loves us more than we love ourselves.

Our Faith is continually being tested by trials both great and small, just as gold is tested in fire. Each difficulty, each disappointment, each heartache is the furnace in which our faith is strengthened and purified. Our Faith is weakened each time we fail to trust in God. We are in for a fall when our own wisdom or sin takes precedence over our love and faith in God.

If instead we turn to God in love and trust, God will not only help us persevere, He will increase and invigorate our faith so we will be able to withstand any trial that comes our way. Sirach 2:6–8 encourages each of us to "**trust God and he will help you; make straight your ways and hope in him. You who fear [revere] the Lord, wait for his mercy; turn not away lest you fall. You, who fear the Lord, trust him, and your reward will not be lost.**"

"**We know that all things work for good for those who love God, who are called according to his purpose.**"__Romans 8:28.

Faith-Building Reflections

"JESUS SAID TO THEM, 'Are you not misled because you do not know the scriptures or the power of God?'"—Mark 12:24.

Don't sell God short. Don't walk around in condemnation. Rejoice! From the cross Jesus said, "It is finished"—John 19:30. He has won our salvation and washed us in His blood. He has taken our infirmities and made us whole and complete. He has canceled all that is against us and disarmed the enemy of his power over us. Repent and believe the Good News! Come before our heavenly Father as a little child and receive your inheritance with praise and thanksgiving. Please God by accepting the victory He has won for us at such a tremendous cost.

When we willingly give everything to Christ, He willingly gives us His grace a hundredfold in return. Anything we declare precious in our own eyes or in the eyes of the world is nothing but trash compared to the richness of the gifts that Christ offers us.

If we expose the darkness of our sins to the light of Christ we find that what was once darkness within us (pride, unbelief, fear, resentment, lukewarmness, etc.) becomes light within us (humility, faith, trust, love, etc).

Dying to self means turning the title of all we are and all we have over to Jesus. We ask what He wants us to do and how He wants us to use the talents, opportunities, and possessions He has given us. Remember, God is able to act in our lives only to the extent to which we let go. Growth in holiness comes through allowing the grace of God to freely work within us. Our childlike openness to God helps us recognize His voice, and our childlike obedience allows us to do as He commands. In return, He brings to our lives the fruits of the Holy Spirit: love, joy, peace, patience, kindness, gentleness, patient endurance, faith, modesty, chastity, and reverence for the Lord.

Remember, "The message of the cross is foolishness to those **who are perishing, but to us who are being saved it is the power of God**"—I Corinthians 1:18. Therefore, never be ashamed of Jesus or of what He desires. Stand up for Him and accept the power of His death and resurrection. Say yes to the Holy Spirit. Because we share in the victory of His cross we will be the most blessed and the most cursed. However, as we walk in Christ's shoes, God will cause us to triumph over all adversities.

The power of God's presence in us must be allowed to transform us into His likeness. We were created in His image but must grow in our likeness to Him. As we experience the reality of God's promises, we will boldly proclaim His mercy to the world with joy and conviction. Then we will come to know the truth, and the truth will set us free.

Beware of those who hold to the form of religion but deny its power. In order to be raised with Christ we must believe in the power of God and rely on His power, not on the wisdom of man. The Spirit of God imparts wisdom and interprets spiritual truths for those who live in the Spirit. The natural man cannot understand Spiritual truths.

When we speak of the natural man we refer to our body, soul, and spirit. Our body consists of our physical structure, our organs and our five senses. Our soul refers to the abstract faculties within us such as our intellect, emotions, memory, will, and imagination. Our spiritual faculties consist of our conscience, intuition, and communion.

Our body, soul, and spirit are hostile toward God and do not submit to God's Will and to His law. Indeed, without God's Spirit at work in us we cannot submit because we have placed our self-centered selves at the center of all our thoughts, actions, and desires. We put ourselves and not God on the throne of our lives.

However, when we invite the Holy Spirit to be the center of our lives and we put Him on the throne, then God can make us a "New Creation." At last, the Holy Spirit can recreate our self-will into His Will. He can transform our rebellious bodies, our soul, and our human spirit into submission to God's Will and into wholeness and holiness.

Feeding On God's Word

SCRIPTURE IS FOOD FOR the soul, life for the spirit, inspiration for the mind, and energy for the body. Scripture renews and energizes.

One of the best ways for Scripture to accomplish the results listed above is for us to "eat" the Word of God daily. Create a storehouse to draw from by committing passages to memory. Then, at a moment's notice you can call forth a quotation to fit the need.

Read a psalm slowly and let the images form in your imagination and speak to you in pictures. Delight in the richness of the images. This practice will lead you to know God in a personal way and to feel the reality of His power, His love, and His majesty.

Scripture also helps us get in touch with our emotions. As you pray the Psalms you will find that they also speak for you. As you read the various Psalms you can label the emotion involved in each. Pick the one you like or need. For example:

Psalm 4 teaches us about confidence.

Psalm 6 teaches us about distress.

Psalm 8 teaches us about awe.

Psalm 10 teaches us about loneliness.

Psalm 13 teaches us about sorrow.

Psalm 18 teaches us about gratitude.

Psalm 22 teaches us about depression.

Psalm 23 teaches us about peace.

Psalm 27 teaches us about security.

Psalm 38 teaches us about repentance.

Psalm 40 teaches us about patience.

Psalm 42 teaches us about longing.

If you take up this practice, God promises He will touch you, bless you, and transform you.

Finding The Path To Truth And Unity

A SILENT RETREAT TITLED A Call to Contemplation proved to be a great blessing. For six days we were surrounded by silence, beauty, and thirty-five loving and caring laypeople along with religious sisters and brothers. During the hours of silence we felt united in love as the silence covered our potential disunity of ideals, beliefs, and values. At the same time, the silence allowed us to center on our Lord Jesus who is the source of truth and unity. However, during the break times, disunity and lack of love raised their ugly voices as we shared our points of view with one another.

If each of us claims to center our lives on Jesus and claims to have the Holy Spirit dwelling in us, why does so much disagreement on issues exist and keep us irritated and separated from each other? Only God knows who's right.

So what can we do to heal our divisions? How can we distinguish truth from error? As Catholics we know and accept the fact that Jesus didn't leave us orphans. He didn't ask us to figure everything out by ourselves. Instead, He left us an institution guided by the Holy Spirit to teach, govern, and sanctify us and to form us into His Mystical Body.

When new ideas and insights present themselves for consideration, how does the Body of Christ deal with this new information, and how do the Church and God's people discern truth from error? How do we come to a decision without abandoning the Spirit of Love who unites us?

I'd like to suggest we follow these guidelines:

Pray for one another and pray for trust, wisdom, love, patience, and openness to all truth.

Study all sides of the question. Pray that those who teach others do so only after careful study and prayer for wisdom.

Beware of fear in all its forms: fear of new ideas and fear of staying locked in the past, fear of grabbing on to the latest will-o'-the-wisp idea, and fear of following the crowd with any and every new fad. Taste, test, and see what fruit the new idea produces.

Remember, it takes time for new ideas to be tried and found to be of value or found to be wanting. Be patient and be open, yet be cautious.

Know and study the heresies of the past. Find out what they were and see if the latest idea may be just another name for something that has already been found erroneous and dangerous to true belief. The devil is fond of dressing lies in different garb at different times.

The Church is a living organism that needs openness to the promptings of the Holy Spirit wherever the truth resides. Also, the Church is the guardian of Faith and needs caution and wisdom in promoting that truth.

Beware of name calling: heretic, traditionalist, liberal, conservative, radical, etc.

Cling to past truths while openly exploring fuller, deeper, and richer understanding of authentic and ancient truth. Seek a blend of the good, the tried, and the true, and trust in the Holy Spirit's guidance. Don't race ahead of approved Church teachings. Remember, the Catholic Church works slowly and methodically. Trust her wisdom and her integrity.

Respond to the call of contemplation where the Spirit speaks to your spirit and confirms or cautions your intellect. Listen in the depths of your spirit not just to the thoughts in your head. Peace is the best indicator of the presence of truth.

Pray and trust God to protect you from all that is potentially harmful, misleading, sinful, untrue, and divisive.

Test for authentic teaching and practices by asking the following questions:

- Does the new idea, insight, information, or truth lead us away for image and symbol and into the never, never land of nirvana?

- Does it draw us away from Christ's Church, which is the source of all goodness, truth, and love?
- Does it draw us into ourselves and away from caring about the concrete world?

If we answer yes to any of these questions it is possible that these ideas can destroy our faith.

However these new ideas etc. can be helpful if they

- Lead us into deeper fraternal charity
- Keep us healthily centered in our state of life
- Lead us to social caring
- Help us grow in the fruits of the Holy Spirit
- Aid us in the acquisition of deeper self knowledge and understanding

If so these new ideas can help us yield more and more to the Spirit's healing and transforming power.

Instead of arguing and name calling, let each of us, alone or with others, reflect silently on the presence of God and seek His truth. Then, the Holy Spirit will be able to lead us together along the path to truth and unity.

Fruitful Deeds

FRUITFULNESS IS SEEING SOMETHING with God's vision, doing something about it with His power, and giving Him the glory for the results. Jesus tells us in Scripture that "**I am the vine, you are the branches. Whoever remains in me and I in him will bear much fruit, because without me you can do nothing**"—John 15:5, and He warns us that we labor in vain unless the Lord works with us.

In sermons we are encouraged to go out and change the world. But we also need to be reminded to pray for God's wisdom in order to discern what the Lord wants us to do. Then it is important to rely on the Holy Spirit to help us accomplish our tasks.

Instead, we usually strike out without waiting to be sure that this act is what God wants us to do, and we forge ahead without praying for guidance. God is seldom in a hurry. When we barge ahead without prayer and reflection it is no wonder our actions bear so little lasting fruit. So we become discouraged and stop trying. Or if we do accomplish something, we tend to become proud.

However, when we do take the time to discern what God is asking us to do and we ask for and rely on His power, we not only see precious fruit blossom, we find the experience truly humbling. This even includes our common, ordinary daily actions. Do them in the Will of God.

Is it really necessary to ask for wisdom and help in each situation and for each decision we are making? Or are our Baptism, Confirmation, and weekly or daily reception of the Eucharist sufficient?

I believe these three Sacraments predispose us to accept the wisdom and the help we seek. However, I also believe that continually seeking wisdom and help in each situation is crucial to our growth in humility and to the fruitfulness of our "good deeds." Remember, true humility comes from constant reliance on God.

Let's consider what God means when He talks about doing "good works" and "bearing much fruit." Daily, many believers and non-believers accomplish good works. The natural goodness in every person makes these deeds possible, and we need to rejoice in all the good that is done by anyone. God can use anything or anyone to bring about good. After all, it is not we who accomplish the good but only God who accomplishes the good through us. By ourselves we can do nothing. Therefore, we should glorify God for any and all good that is done. If every breath we take, every act we do, every thought we think etc. is done in the Divine Will God receives all the glory.

Remember how Jesus reprimanded the disciples when they complained about those who were casting out demons in Jesus' name but who weren't part of their company? Jesus said to them, **"Do not prevent him. There is no one who performs a mighty deed in my name who can at the same time speak ill of me"**—Mark 9:38. **"For whoever is not against us is for us"**—Mark 9:40. Notice that they were acting in Jesus' name.

There is a significant difference between the type of good works that can be accomplished by someone who is relying on their own power and by someone who actively sought the Spirit's help and who relied on the Spirit's power and His gifts. Through serious prayer and openness to the Spirit we grow in the cardinal virtues of temperance, fortitude, prudence, and justice in order to cooperate with grace and grow in the ability to use our "talents" to do good works. In Matthew 25:14–30 Jesus speaks about using our talents for the good of others. In the Catholic Faith we refer to these as the corporal and spiritual works of mercy. The closer we grow to God through prayer the more God is able to work through our actions and the greater will be the effect of our acts

For instance, the healing of memories or inner healing can only be accomplished through the power of the Holy Spirit. This gift of healing enables us to cooperate with the Holy Spirit in order to bring healing to the past hurts that so cripple a person's ability to function in a holy, healthful way. Once these wounds are healed an individual knows the power of God is real. These are the truly fruitful deeds, the good works that have lasting value and really bring glory to God. Or what about setting someone free from the oppressive forces of evil by speaking a word of wisdom, of knowledge, or spiritual insight to the needy soul, or proclaiming the Good News in Jesus' name to someone who is lost?

Yet time and time again those who are in these ministries report dramatic, life-producing changes in people. Unfortunately, these areas of healing and deliverance are often neglected and ignored.

Perhaps we need to ask God to increase our understanding and our faith regarding the importance of the gifts of the Holy Spirit with which we can touch, transform, and set people free from so many of life's difficulties. We need to expand our horizons concerning how much God wants to do for us and to grow to trust that He truly wants to heal us and set us free.

Remember the healing of the boy with a demon in Mark 9:14–29. It tells about the father who brought his son to Jesus to expel a mute spirit from the boy. The man complained that he had asked the disciple to expel him, but they were unable to do so. Jesus replied to the crowd, **"What an unbelieving lot you are!"** Then after Jesus had further questioned the father, the man said to Jesus, **"If, out of the kindness of your heart you can do anything to help us, please do!"** Jesus said, **"If you can? Everything is possible to a man who trusts."** The boy's father immediately exclaimed, **"I do believe! Help my lack of trust!"** Then the disciples asked Him, **"Why could we not drive it out?"** He said to them, **"This kind can only be driven out by prayer."**

- How about us? Don't we also need to cry out?
- Lord, deliver me from self-sufficiency.
- I do believe! Lord, help my lack of trust.
- Lord, deliver me from "do-it-yourself-ism."
- Lord, deliver me from rugged individualism.
- Lord, give me the desire to possess and use Your gifts.
- Lord, teach me how to use Your gifts effectively.

Take Time To Ponder #2

IT'S MOST BENEFICIAL IF your reflections are written down and pondered often.

- Has unanswered prayer destroyed or weakened my faith?
- Do I understand that unanswered prayer is perhaps a type of suffering that can produce virtue in me?
- What could be the cause of a specific prayer being unanswered?
- Do I believe that God always answers me but in His own way and time?
- Am I missing the hidden answers because I am looking in the wrong place?
- Am I so busy looking for results that I don't give the seed a chance to grow and blossom?
- Jesus planted seeds and even His often fell on poor soil. Should I say "Thanks" anyway and wait patiently for God to improve the soil?
- Would it be better to petition God, to trust in His love, and to praise Him for the answer even though I don't perceive it? Would this help me grow in faith and open me more readily to accept God's answer?
- Do I pray expectantly?
- What kind or prayers are most pleasing to God's heart?

Our God is a loving, faithful friend who always answers our prayers in the way that is best for each of us. Remember also that man's free will is always operable and can block God's greatest gifts from reaching us. Praying with a repentant heart is the prayer most readily and easily heard by God.

Getting Off Life's
Teeter-Totter

HOW WONDERFUL IT IS when our lives are in balance. Unfortunately, most of us find we live a "teeter-totter life," one end up and the other end down. Right? There's always too much of one thing and not enough of another: work/play; sleep/lack of sleep; prayer/lack of prayer; boredom/confusion; togetherness/loneliness; overeating/dieting; and so forth. From my experience, it seems that the cause is really quite simple—we put last things first and first things last.

Time after time I have found the following to be true. When I spend the first hour of my day (or some time during the night) engaging in prayer, Scripture study, spiritual reading, and journaling, the rest of my day falls in line. However, when I start my day doing everything else first, I end up skimping or forgetting to take quality time to speak to and listen to Our Lord. Then, as the saying goes, "The faster I go the be hinder I get," and my day is soon out of kilter.

I constantly have to remind myself that even if it doesn't seem reasonable, all will go well if I pray first and then do everything else. Time seems to have a way of expanding.

The second secret of getting off the teeter-totter of life, which also doesn't seem reasonable, is to Pay God first and then pay the rest of the bills. Tithing isn't logical according to the worldly wise, but according to the way God runs His universe it is logical and does work.

It's simply a matter of having our priorities in order. Jesus says **"seek first the kingdom [of God] and his righteousness, and all these things will be given you besides. Do not worry about tomorrow; tomorrow will take care of itself"**—Matt 6:33–34.

Go Stand In The Gap

WE'VE ALL BEEN TOLD not to criticize another until, as the Indians say, "You've walked in the other man's moccasins." Scripture also tells us in Exodus 17:9–11 how Moses stood in the gap and prayed while Joshua and his men battled against the Amaleks. When Moses held up his hands in prayer, Israel prevailed, but when he let his hands down and stopped interceding, the Amaleks prevailed.

The power of intercessory prayer comes when we truly enter into another person's suffering. The most effective way to pray for someone or for some situation is to stand in the gap. That is, to pray in the place of that person or that situation.

Consider for example the case of someone who had deliberately turned away from God and through sexual promiscuity has contracted AIDS. Perhaps your prayer might sound like this:

"God, I feel so sick today. I feel tired and frightened and alone. I know I brought this on myself; therefore, I have no one else to blame. I was warned that promiscuity was physically dangerous, but I closed my ears and kept giving in to lust. I knew it was sinful, but I didn't care, because I neither knew You nor loved You. O, Lord, why was I so rebellious? Jesus, please forgive me and help me forgive the person who infected me. Give me the courage to face the future. Help me offer You my pain in atonement for my sins and the sins of others who refuse to hear Your voice. And Lord in your mercy please heal me."

As we cry out with the voice of the one who suffers, as we place ourselves in their moccasins and stand in the gap with arms raised in prayer and praise, the destructive effects of criticism, anger, and despair are released and are replaced with the healthy fruit of compassion, understanding, and hope. Standing in the gap unites us in love. It enables us to feel the agony. It empowers and puts flesh on our prayer. Remember, God always hears the "cry of the poor." So be poor and embrace the pain of your "brother or sister." Prayer is more powerful than condemnation.

God Invites Us To Fulfillment

(Isaiah 55 Summarized)

GOD INVITES US TO receive His grace. He says that all who thirst should come to Christ, the "water of life." Don't waste your time and effort on things that won't satisfy. Instead, draw close to God, and you shall be filled with the very thing for which you are searching—love, fulfillment, peace, and joy.

He goes on to say that if we do come to Him we will have everything that God promised David. God made him a leader, a witness, and a commander of nations. Like David, many will come to us to be led to the same fulfillment. This is possible because God will glorify us.

Do we honestly seek the Lord? Do we go where we can find Him? Do we call out to Him in our need? Isaiah says that if scoundrels and wicked men forsake their ways and turn to God, they will find that He is generous in forgiving. After all, His ways are not our ways and His thoughts are not our thoughts. Everything the Lord does, every word He speaks does His Will and produces the result He intends. If we are truly in Him and He uses us to speak His word, we will see results that will glorify our Father. Then, filled with God's grace, we shall go forth in joy and come back in peace. Wherever we go all shall sing and clap their hands. Joy shall replace sorrow, peace shall replace anxiety and fear, and we shall be a sign of God's presence in the world.

Has The Power Gone?

The Early Church:

"And now, Lord, take note of their threats, and enable your servants to speak your word with all boldness, as you stretch forth [your] hand to heal, and signs and wonders are done through the name of your holy servant Jesus. As they prayed, the place where they were gathered shook, and they were all filled with the Holy Spirit and continued to speak the word of God with boldness. The community of believers was of one heart and mind, and no one claimed that any of his possessions was his own, but they had everything in common"—Acts 4:29–32.

The Church Today:

How DO WE COMPARE to the above quotation from the Acts of the Apostles? Is anyone threatening us because we proclaim before the entire world, our friends included, that Jesus Christ is Lord? Or do we compromise our beliefs; water them down so they're acceptable to anyone and everyone?

Do our lives reflect Gospel values? Or are we so enmeshed in the culture around us that neither those inside the Church or outside know we are disciples of Jesus?

Do cures and signs and wonders happen in our midst? Or are we so accustomed to relying on our own power that we forget to ask God for help and to pray expectantly in the name of Jesus?

When we pray as a community, does the Church vibrate with God's power, and are our hearts set on fire with love? Or are we "dry bones" who merely put in time in order to guarantee our own salvation? Do we exhibit a half-dead faith, and do we lack a love relationship with God as well?

Are we so filled with the Holy Spirit that we speak God's Word to each other and to outsiders with confidence? Or are we embarrassed to even mention the name of Jesus except in quiet prayer? Perhaps we don't even mention His name at all if Jesus isn't a personal friend and the center of our life.

Are we united in one mind and one heart because we are centered on the Lord? Or are we so divided among ourselves that the mere mention of any number of topics brings dissent, debate, labeling, and partisanship?

If someone was tempted to arrest us for being a Christian, would there be enough evidence to convict us?

Let's take the words of Scripture to heart. Let's open our lives to the Holy Spirit. Let's stop hiding behind our fears of each other. Let's seek unity by accepting and following the teachings Jesus given to us through the Church which Jesus established to teach, govern and sanctify mankind.

If we did these things we would then reflect the dynamic presence of Christ as the early Church did as quoted in Acts 4: 29–32. The power of the Holy Spirit is available to us just for the asking. Repent! Believe! Ask for this power and then act with it! The Holy Spirit is waiting for us to do so.

No! The power has not gone!

We just need to tap into it.

Spiritual Friendship

EACH OF US IS called to spiritual friendship with another and to an intimate relationship with God. Unfortunately, our failure rate in both is probably high. Success in building these relationships lies in our ability to listen openly, to understand, to accept another's point of view, and to wait patiently for change in ourselves and in the other.

In Thomas Hart's wonderful book <u>The Art of Christian Listening</u>, the author points out that "although all our concerns and all aspects of our lives are the basis for spiritual friendship, true spiritual friendship cannot take place unless each partner is in touch with God through prayer. Then, as we dialogue with our spiritual friend, we will begin to see ourselves and all of life from God's point of view rather than from our own ..."

Hart suggests we take heed of the following reminders if our prayer is to be successful:

- "Don't try to make something beautiful for God, like having good, holy thoughts and warm, loving feelings.
- Don't worry if your attentiveness is filled with distractions.
- Don't seek a religious experience.
- Don't give up because God seems so distant and disinterested.
- Don't give up when prayer appears to be unproductive."

On page fifty-four the author says that "prayer is rather being yourself before God, coming as you are, dialoguing with Him from your present situation, not putting on a face and manufacturing appropriate thoughts and feelings, but simply working with both the positive and negative thoughts and feelings that are there."

He says spiritual friends and spiritual directors must remember:

- to be good listeners and keep all that is shared confidential;
- to walk beside the other and be a true friend;
- to love your companion unconditionally, thus enabling your friend to believe in himself and to rejoice in his uniqueness;
- to be yourself with no facades;
- to be willing to agree and confirm, or to simply understand and to accept without condemnation;
- that the helper is not responsible for the other person's life;
- that the helper is not there to remove the problem and the pain;
- that the helper need not necessarily be wiser, holier, or have greater experience, though these might be considerable assets;
- that the helper is not to make the other into a different person.

Hundredfold Return

WHAT A WONDERFUL COUNTRY we live in. What a wonderful age in which to live. Everything we ever dreamed of possessing is virtually ours for the choosing. Whether it's the smallest non-essential gimmick or the grandest electronic convenience, the fastest mode of transportation or the most beautiful item of clothing can be ours. Yet, how empty we are.

How different are the heartbreaking stories of destitution we see on television, read about in the press or hear about from those who have seen it with their own eyes. Perhaps, some of us have personally experienced poverty or worked with those who live in it daily.

Sometime ago, I read an article whose message haunted me. The article told about a Catholic nun who was given permission to leave her cloister during the week to tend to the needs of the poor. Much to her delight she found a beautiful and unexpected reality. What she found was a suffering, but joyful people who were eager to share with one another. She found people who exhibited a sense of freedom in which to enjoy each other and the few material things they owned. It seemed that in spite of their lack of material goods, they possessed more of what really matters: they seemed loving and full of life. Better yet, notice the joy and freedom apparent in the lives of those who choose voluntary poverty, i.e. Mother Therese of Calcutta

From Numbers 18: 21-32 & Genesis 28:22 "…**Of everything you give me, I will faithfully return a 10th part to you**" we learn that God asks us to give a tithe of the first fruits of our labor. That is, to give the first 10 percent of our gross income to alleviate the sufferings of those less fortunate than ourselves and/or to those who are engaged in building up the Body of Christ.

Those who have been faithful to this tithing principle have found that God is truly a generous God who is faithful to His Word. Those who give joyfully and generously will never be outdone in generosity.

I Love My Pet

I REALLY LOVE MY pet, but it doesn't respond to my affection. I'm not sure if my pet would love me more if I gave it rules to guide its behavior. Or perhaps I should just let it do as it pleases. Which way would gain me its love?

Does it love me more or less when I make it tow the mark and behave? I give it treats and shower favors upon it, but it still ignores me, and I am brokenhearted. I feel sad and lonely when my pet turns away from me and pays more attention to someone or something instead of me.

Then one day, I was thinking about how Jesus must feel when I ignore Him, my greatest love and friend. How cruel and thoughtless I am to do this to my God who became a human being, who suffered brutally and died an ignominious death so I could have the gift of happiness in heaven for all eternity, if I choose to take His gift.

Forgive me, Lord, for all the hurt I have caused You. How much You must sorrow because of my lack of love and appreciation. Please, dear Lord, forgive me! I promise to love You more each day, and I gratefully accept Your great and eternal gift of love and salvation.

Invitation To The Quiet Life

No matter where I am or to whom I speak, the topic invariably centers on questions about one's daily activities, accomplishments, responsibilities, and future goals. I come away feeling impressed as well as overwhelmed, depressed, and yes, even a little guilty when I hear about the many things that people are doing and accomplishing. They seem to have a great passion for life and all that the world has to offer. I admire them, yet I wonder if their life is really any more valid than the life of someone who has chosen the quiet life of solitude, silence, and prayer—where "being" is considered equally as important as "doing."

Perhaps we need to ask ourselves some hard questions:

- Do I feel worthwhile because of what I do, or do I feel worthwhile because I simply am?
- Is all the hectic, stress-filled activity that fills my day really God's Will for my life, or am I keeping busy to fill my emptiness?
- Am I withdrawing from the hustle and bustle of life because I am seeking God, or am I withdrawing in order to escape responsibility?

Perhaps the answers rest on the fact that any lifestyle is valid only to the extent to which one seeks the Will of God through prayerful communication with the Father each day and at each turn and at decision.

I would like to suggest that we evaluate the need for the quiet life in terms of today's society for both those who choose the active life and those who choose the contemplative life. For the truth of the matter is that taking time for solitude, silence, and prayer refreshes and invigorates us no matter which lifestyle we choose. It gets us in touch with the source of all enlightenment, happiness, peace, and fulfillment. St. Augustine wrote that after living a life of running away from God, he discovered that "our hearts are restless until they rest in Thee, my God"—Confessions by Saint Augustine.

The Church has long recognized the validity of the quiet life for those who retired to the desert in search of God and those who chose to live in contemplative orders with others. Each spent their lives in solitude, silence, prayer, study, and manual labor. In love they sought God, and God in turn used them as channels of grace for others. These wise and holy people were highly respected and sought after for their wisdom. They were like the calm in the midst of a stormy sea as they "plugged" their lives into the source of all life and brought that life to others.

I contend that today the clergy and laity are also called to this place in God's Kingdom on Earth, each of us adapting the ideal to one's own particular circumstance.

I suggest one might begin by considering the following ten possibilities:

- Shut off all auditory distractions such as radio, TV, stereo, etc.
- Eliminate all unnecessary phone calls, and keep the necessary ones short and to the point. Don't gab or gossip.
- Talk only when necessary. When you do talk, converse only to edify, to be helpful, or to bring joy to another. James 3:6 says, "**The tongue is also a fire. It exists among our members as a world of malice, defiling the whole body and setting the entire course of our lives on fire, itself set on fire by Gehenna.**"
- Keep your thoughts on your work when required. When thinking is not required, pray familiar prayers, talk with God in your own words, or pray in the Spirit.
- Take time to feed your spirit by praying and studying Scripture.

- Read the works of spiritual writers of the past and the present to inspire you and cause you to grow in holiness.
- Drive away negative, destructive, and worthless thoughts by calling on Jesus and Mary for help. Remember, Scripture instructs us to think only on those things that are true and good and beautiful.
- If you feel lonely, remember that God is always with you. Practice the presence of God.

I would like to suggest that we evaluate the need for the quiet life in terms of today's society for both those who choose the active life and those who choose the contemplative life.

- Mind your own business, not anyone else's.
- Eliminate clutter from your life by doing only those things which God asks of you and keep only those things He wants you to have. Romans 8:5 says, **"For those who live according to the flesh are concerned with the things of the flesh, but those who live according to the spirit with the things of the spirit."**
- Living the quiet life is far from escapism. In fact, as you draw deeper into this life you will become sensitive to the sorrows and joys of others. God's point of view will more readily become your own and His love and care more a part of your very being.
- At the same time, others will cast you as an outsider, not quite "with it," or perhaps a bit peculiar. "False guilt" will cause you to feel that you ought to be out there "doing" something for fear that people will think you are uncaring and self-centered. Guilt, loneliness, and doubt will suggest that your motives are not pure.
- But don't fear. Great peace and tranquility will be yours. Memorable moments of inspiration will be yours too as you sense God calling you to yield more and more of your time to Him alone. And last but not least, you

will have time to do all things well for the honor and glory of God.

These thoughts are well confirmed by Saint Bernard, who once wrote a tract titled De Consideratione, concerning meditation, which Thomas Merton quoted in his book The Last Of The Fathers.

"The importance of De Consideratione lies in its stress on the interior life and on the essential primacy of contemplation over action ... the interior life ought, by rights, be preferred to exterior action. Action is a necessity, and we are in fact prevented from remaining always in silence, contemplation, study and prayer. But action is only valid if [it] is nourished by a deep interior life. [Our actions] should not absorb so much of our time and energy that meditation, prayer and silent reflection become impossible. ... The fact that our works are done in service of God is not enough, by itself, to prevent us from losing our interior life if we let [our acts of service] devour all our time and all our strength. Work is good and necessary, but too much of it renders the soul insensitive to spiritual values, hardens the heart against prayer and divine things. It requires a serious effort and courageous sacrifice to resist this hardness of heart." St. Bernard writes that this advice is "valuable for all prelates and for all men ..."

God invites us into the quiet life where He can speak to our hearts. He yearns for an intimate relationship with each of us. Be sure to RSVP to His invitation. "I accept with pleasure, dear Jesus, Your kind invitation to draw closer to You."

Meditation On Pain

Jesus falls a second time.

Once again Jesus stumbles and falls.

The movement of the heavy beam bears down on his raw and bleeding flesh.

It tears and bruises his tender skin and causes the crown of thorns to pierce deeper into his sensitive body.

Salty sweat seeps into His open wounds. It stings and burns His sensitive body.

The boisterous spectators who line the narrow street jostle and rub against Jesus, making it almost impossible for Him to drag His body forward.

At last, weakened by the loss of blood, exhausted by the throbbing pain, thrown off balance by the crowd, and overcome with the pain of misunderstanding, rejection, and abandonment, Jesus collapses onto the hot, dusty cobblestones.

Jesus' love for us and His devotion to the Father's Will drove Him to rise from the second fall and complete His mission, our salvation.

All He asks of us is **to "take up our cross daily and follow Him"**—Luke 9:23.

It's Like Planting A Garden

"Johnny, before you plant the seeds, remember to till the soil," his father said as Johnny bent over and tried to press the seeds into the resistant soil.

"Maybe Dad's right. This ground feels like a rock."

So with spade, trowel, fingers, and rake Johnny worked the soil until at last it was receptive to the seeds. He watered the garden daily in order to soften the seeds so the plant inside could break through its outer covering, send down roots, and eventually develop stems, leaves, and fruit.

Evangelization, like planting a garden, takes planning and hard work. God provides the seed and God produces the fruit. However, under the guidance and the power of the Holy Spirit, we are the ones who choose the garden spot, prepare the soil, plant the seed, water the garden, pull out the weeds, and scare away the thieves who come to steal and destroy.

Choosing the best garden spot requires careful study. Likewise, in evangelization, prayerful discernment helps us determine where God desires us to plant the Gospel seed. Then, before planting God's Word, cultivation is necessary. This is done by establishing a friendship based on trust and mutual respect with the person chosen. Confidentiality is also a crucial ingredient on which to build any friendship. Everything we think, everything we do, and everything we say proclaims the Gospel message. Therefore, it must be God's love and God's righteousness, not our condemnation and self-righteousness that radiates from us.

Once the Good News has been planted in the garden, we water it with abundant prayer, for without the life-giving water of the Holy Spirit our labor will be in vain.

Like a good gardener, we pull out the weeds of error, resistance, and doubt with gentle correction and with patient and careful teaching. We also fertilize our garden and ourselves by encounters with Christ through the Mass, the Sacraments, daily Scripture reading, prayer, good example, sound teaching, and encouragement from a caring Christian community.

If we have allowed the Holy Spirit and God's wisdom to aid us in our work, our garden will grow to maturity, and abundant fruit will soon be ready for the harvester.

Joined Together In Christ

A HEALTHY CHRISTIAN COMMUNITY is as necessary to our growth and maturity as followers of Christ as clean air is to good health. However, in order for the community to benefit anyone, it must be completely centered on the Lord and constantly seeking His wisdom as we listen to Him and follow the promptings of His Spirit.

If the Lord is allowed to build the community, we will see its members grow strong in service to others. This service will be marked by the presence of the fruits of the Holy Spirit. Transformation of individual lives will become evident as the healing freedom of Jesus' love begins to permeate the lives of others.

On the other hand, if we center our lives on ourselves, anything or anyone other than Jesus, or if our efforts are concentrated on pursuits other than seeking to glorify God alone, then division within the community will follow.

Likewise, if the fruits of the Holy Spirit—charity (love), joy, peace, patience, kindness, gentleness, longsuffering, mildness, faith, modesty, chastity, and fear of the Lord—are not evident, then it is doubtful whether this congregation is truly committed to establishing a community centered on Jesus or that it is allowing the Holy Spirit to guide it.

The growth and the maturity of an individual or a community results only to the degree to which each individual Christian is willing to yield himself or herself to the Lord at each moment and in each circumstance. The more one yields oneself, the more one finds that their love and their service to others increases. When one stops loving or stops reaching out to others one begins to die.

Each of us must look at our own lives and ask ourselves the following questions:

- Do I really have the Holy Spirit within me?
- Are the fruits of the Spirit evident in my life?
- Who or what is the center of my life?
- Do I seek to know Jesus or do I seek other goals?
- Do other interests keep me from letting Jesus take over?
- Does negativism, cynicism, or criticism block my love?
- Does my lack of forgiveness create bondage in my relationships with others?
- Jesus says, "Let me live in you. Give me your life and stop taking it back. I want to love you, to bring you peace and to help you in all things."
- When Jesus truly lives in the members of a Christian community, the members find themselves willing to share their time, their talents and their material possessions with one another. When each person pitches in everyone reaps the benefits, and that's when the community truly reflects Christ to the world.

Journey Into Truth

Where, pray tell, did it all begin? In the womb? In the crib? In the sandbox? At school? In church? Or was it a particular relationship that sparked the seed of discontent? Was it the germ of an idea that later blossomed into a wrong turn of thought, a mistaken idea of faith, a lopsided view of God, self, and the world?

Prove yourself! Prove yourself, the thought beckoned. Torment began. As the years progressed, the actions and reactions that she performed to prove herself lovable, good, and worthy continued unabated.

The child responded. "I'm not pretty enough! I'm not smart enough! I'm not worthy enough! I'm not talented enough!" Lies. Lies. All of them lies.

"If I do more. If I study more. If I work harder. If I keep silent and respond 'yes' to all their calls. Perhaps then I shall be worthy. Worthy to enter the Kingdom. Worthy to be called His child. Worthy of the respect of others." And so she struggled harder to be made worthy.

Finally, exhausted, harried, frustrated, and unprepared once again to do the task at hand, the woman sobbed. Sobbed until a dark cloud thoroughly encompassed her. It sucked her down, down, down into the pit of despair. The darkness stifled reason. It told lies of unworthiness and failure. It made unrelenting attacks and produced hideous visions.

This time proved worse than any previous time. This time all doors seemed closed. No one understood. Her children seemed terrified. Her husband was bewildered. How could this be? they asked. She's always so happy, so healthy, so talented, so loving, so giving, so admired, so loved.

"Talk it out. Talk to someone who understands what's happened. Stop doing. Stop going. Stop trying to prove you are worthy," the voice warned. "Count the minutes. Count the hours. Count the time it takes to do the day's chores. How much time remains?"

Relief. Blessed relief. Relief from pressure. Time to think. Time to pray. Time to read. Time to complete the tasks assigned. Time to do them well.

Then His words came to her: **"Come to me all you who are heavily burdened and I will give you rest. I am the Way, the Truth and the Light"**—Matthew 11:28. When you come to truly know Me and trust Me, I will set you free. You cannot save yourself. Only I can save you, Jesus tells us so often.

Then darkness lifted. Light and truth appeared. Balance was restored. Joy, Peace, Wisdom, Freedom, and Healthy Self-Love returned. Truth broke through.

Joy Of Submission

GOD MADE ALL THINGS and keeps them in existence. He knows all things that have been, are now, and will be. He gave us free will along with many powers and abilities. Although God has foreseen, planned, and permitted whatever happens to us, He has bestowed upon us the intelligence to judge and the will to choose. But our choices are not always what are best for us.

God's choices, on the other hand, are always in our best interest, even when it involves suffering, pain, and loss. It's wise to ask Him for advice before making a decision. But it is even more important to desire whatever God desires, to obey His commandments, and to cooperate with His grace. This is called abandonment to Divine Providence.

When we place all things at God's feet and trust Him to act in our best interest, He will not disappoint us, even when His answer differs from our desire. Submitting to God's Will and relaxing in His loving care will chase our fears and worries away. Even if our plans and efforts fail, we need not complain or rebel because we understand that God always knows what's best for us. Remember, Romans 8:28 says, **"We know that all things work for good for those who love God, who are called according to his purpose."** Therefore, praise God in all circumstances

Keys To Freedom

GOD LOVES EACH OF us with an everlasting and perfect love. He desires to help us with all the problems we face. He cares even about our messed up, sin-filled lives. He wants to set us free to be happy and fulfilled. He doesn't want us to go through life heavily burdened and in despair. His heart aches when He sees us unhappy and in pain because sin is wearing us down.

Most of the time our lives merely reflect the degradation of the society in which we live. Maybe we have bought the lies we are bombarded with day in and day out. Maybe we have sowed the seeds of our own destruction. Maybe we are reaping the harvest of our own iniquity and our lack of dependence on God.

Take a look at the sinfulness around us: lust and sexual perversion, selfishness and greed, hate and violence, addictions to destructive substances and behaviors, the slaughter of hundreds of innocent unborn children, and the rampant acceptance of the occult and false beliefs. These are but a few evidences that indicate we are not walking as children of the Light, which is Christ Jesus.

The fruits of our actions are evident and they show up in the diseases of our bodies, our souls, and our spirits: fear; anxiety; depression; alienation; corruption; increase of mental, emotional, and psychological misery; as well as financial uncertainty to name but a few. The self-righteous as well as the partakers of evil are equally guilty. Unfortunately, the innocent as well as the guilty will suffer if our institutions and our nations collapse from the weight of our collective sin.

Will our cities, towns, and institutions be destroyed like the Biblical cities of Sodom and Gomorrah? Or, like Nineveh, to whom Jonah preached, will they repent and turn to the source of life and be saved?

It's the principalities and the powers of darkness, as well as our own weakened human nature we are fighting against, not one another. God has called us to love one another, to care for each other, and to pray against and make reparation for the all the evil in the world.

Jesus came to save us from all this. He came to give us life to the full and everlasting happiness with Him forever in heaven. So why do we not turn to Jesus, who waits with open, forgiving arms? He knows us better that we know ourselves. He is the source of all that is good and true and beautiful. He is the source of all peace and joy and unity. He is the source of all love and forgiveness. He loves our villages, towns, and cities, all our nations and our cultures and each unique aspect of our lives.

If we pray for the humility to see ourselves as we really are,

If we turn to Him and repent,

If we desire to do His Will not ours,

We will be reconciled to one another in truth and love.

These are the keys to freedom, joy, peace, and fulfillment.

"In you our ancestors trusted; they trusted and you rescued them. To you they cried out and they escaped; in you they trusted and were not disappointed"—Psalm 22:5–6.

Take Time To Ponder #3

IT IS MOST BENEFICIAL, if your reflections are written down and pondered often.

- Do I have faith in the openness of the person for whom I'm praying?
- Do I see myself as I truly am or do I see myself with "rose colored glasses"? Do I ask God to help me see my true self?
- How often do I pray for myself and others for the grace to grow in faith, to repent, to forgive, and for the wisdom to see things as God sees them?
- Before I pray for someone, do I ask God to show me what He wants me to request for this person?
- God said, **"Ask and it will be given to you; seek and you shall find; knock and the door will be opened to you"**—Matthew 7:7. Do I ask and seek?
- How do my negative attitude and my lack of faith keep God from helping me?
- Individual and corporate sin is the cause of suffering and unanswered prayer. How has my lack of love kept someone from opening their heart to God?
- Do I have a contrite heart and a broken spirit? Read Psalm 51.
- What does letting go mean to me? To what am I clinging?

Recall the story of the Israelites. Contemplate their courage, faith, patience, obedience, and disobedience in their relationship with God as they waited for the promised redeemer. What does this say to me?

- Have I meditated on the story of the Israelites and placed myself in their story? Am I also disobedient like they were?

Like Conversation Prayer Flows

WHEN OUR MOTHER AND father entertained friends, my sister and I would sit on the stairs and listen to the conversation in the living room. Adult conversation intrigued us. When we heard one of our parents coming, we'd race upstairs and jump into bed. As we lay there in the dark, we tried to untangle the web of conversation. We weren't so much interested in what they'd said but in how adult conversation moved so smoothly from one subject to another.

Years later, while at "silent" prayer one day, I was reminded of this childhood experience. I became conscious of the fact that when praying in the Spirit, not with the mind, my conversation with God flowed from one type of prayer to another. It resembled the same kind of flowing conversation that took place between my parents and their friends.

If you are interested in pursuing this type of prayer, here are a few suggestions of how to get started:

First get comfortable. Quiet your mind and relax your body, like a rag doll. Be pliable under the Spirit's guidance. You may begin by using the gift of praying in tongues, by quietly repeating the name of Jesus, or reciting the "Jesus prayer" over and over: *Jesus, Son of the Living God, have mercy on me, a sinner.*

By letting go in this way, your mind will become quiet and you will soon find yourself entering into deep prayer and silence. The Holy Spirit will guide your conversation with God without any particular conscious decisions on your part. Your human spirit will be united with God's Spirit in prayer.

As you continue in silent prayer you may notice that you are moving from one mode of prayer to another. Any one of the following types of communication may be part of this conversation with God: singing, silence, and praise, talking over a problem, mentioning a particular intention, recalling a verse from Scripture or some inspiring or helpful idea, praying in tongues, or repeating the name of Jesus or some phrase over and over, even using a memorized prayer.

Prayer is conversation with God. It's two-sided. Don't be rude and do all the talking. Give God time to speak to your heart.

It's interesting to experience how this quiet way of prayer, like adult conversation, flows silently from one type of prayer to another under the Spirit's gentle guidance. Even silence is acceptable. Apparently, all one needs to do is to place oneself in Jesus' hands and relax.

It may take time to learn to let go and to yield to the Spirit's promptings, but it's worth it. You will find it a most enjoyable way to spend time with your best and most intimate friend. You may even fall asleep in God's loving arms, and that's all right too, if sleep comes of its own accord.

"Londonderry Aire"

Words by Father Oliver Walsh
O Lord my God, I long to sing your praises:
O Lord my God, with songs of love and joy.
The night is past
And now at last
'Tis I, 'Tis I, must live my life anew.

Stay with me Lord.
And guide me on the journey.
Into my heart your Spirit sends each day.
My heart in Christ immerse 'til it is burning
With thoughts of thanks, adoration, prayer and praise.

O Lord my God, I long to sing your praises
For being God immortal, great and free
For souring far
Above this world of smallness
Where our small lives compare Thy "immensity".

All glory, honor
Praise and adoration
Be yours always, O universal King.
And may your Son, Lord Jesus with His Spirit
Draw all men to himself in faith and love again.

A song of praise I raise to you Lord Jesus
A song of praise to you I'll always sing.
You've given your life
For me

A nothing sinner.
But now you rule within my heart as king.

Your tender love I deeply cherish
Your deep concern
And special care for me.
I give to you the only thing I relish
My will with all its longing to be free.

Lord, Give Me Faith

Lord, empty me like an old tin can.
Then fill me with FAITH
Which is
As strong as an oak
As fragrant as a rose
As durable as a diamond
And as fertile as black soil.
Make me as
Powerful as an ocean
Productive as a beaver
Grace-filled as a dogwood tree
Joyful as a song bird.
Then, Lord, empower me
With your gifts and your grace
So you and I together can transform the world
As I sing your praise
And manifest your presence.
ALLELUIA

Loving, Bearing, Sharing

Jesus said we must:
- Love one another as He has loved us,
- Bear one another's burdens, and
- Share each other's joys.

THE CLOSER WE DRAW to the Blessed Trinity, the easier we will find ourselves united in loving service to one another, sharing the Good News in joy, and bearing one another's burdens in love. Through this deep sharing and caring the Christian community moves from being a purely bureaucratic structure of hard-hearted, self-complacent individuals into the living reality of Christ present in today's society. But fear holds us back: fear of revealing ourselves to one another, fear of rejection, fear of becoming involved, and fear of losing control of our time and talent.

It takes time, effort, and willingness to be inconvenienced for the sake of another. It takes time to really listen and not just hear. It takes great love to respect another's opinion and not manipulate another into our way of thinking and doing. It takes patience to wait for the Lord to speak to someone's heart. It takes courage and faith to watch someone freely walk the wrong direction, trusting that God is in charge and that He will turn them around.

It takes compassion and selflessness to deal with a suffering brother or sister. It takes grace to realize that true Christian community is not a luxury but a necessity.

Pray for the grace to love, share, and bear with one another so the world can say once again, "See how those Christians love one another."

Mini Reflection On Joy

JOY IN FOLLOWING CHRIST is a theme threaded throughout the epistle of St. Paul to the Philippians. However, before we can rejoice in this joy, we must repent. Repentance begets forgiveness, and forgiveness begets joy.

St. Paul points out the following ten joys of being a Christian:

Joy of Prayer: To sit quietly beside Jesus. To speak to him as a friend. To listen as He speaks to us in the stillness of our hearts.

Joy When Jesus Is Preached: For how can anyone come to know Christian joy unless they hear the Good News?

Joy in Faith: It is said that "seeing is believing," but in the Christian life we must believe in order to understand, and then we begin to see clearly.

Joy in Unity: How miserable we feel when we are at odds with one another. How we ache because of the separation that comes because we build walls of discord, misunderstanding, and lack of trust in one another's integrity.

Joy of Suffering for Jesus' Sake: The more the Saints suffered because of their faith the more they rejoiced.

Joy of Knowing a Loved One Is in Christ: Notice how anxiety fades and unity is restored when someone we love returns to Jesus.

Joy of Christian Hospitality: As we see Christ in one another, how much more readily do we open our doors and our hearts to that person?

Joy in the Lord: When Jesus is the center of our life, everything else falls into place.

Joy in Bringing the Good News to Another: Freely sharing our Faith turns fear into joy and growth of virtue and belief into motion.

New Life Unfolds Unobserved

ONE SUMMER I WATCHED a fascinating time-lapsed film describing the life of a tree that had fallen in the forest and how the tree ended in total decay.

Through time-lapsed, microscopic photography I watched as countless natural predators aided in the decaying process. The tree lay dormant for years. It remained open and vulnerable to the passage of time and to nature's miraculous way of bringing new life forth from death.

It would be interesting if we could review our own process of spiritual growth or demise through this same kind of photography. The journaling process is the closest we can come, but journaling is too subjective. The only way we can really understand our status before God would be through God's point of view.

"For you have died, and your life is hidden now with Christ in God."—Colossians 3:3. Like the fallen tree, if we are to grow and nourish others, we must **"Stop lying to one another, since you have taken off the old self with its practices and have put on the new self, which is being renewed, for knowledge, in the image of its creator"**—Colossians 3:9–10.

It is we who do the lying still, the putting aside. It is God who sends the transforming circumstances to cause our false self to decay and the new man, the true self, made in the image and likeness of God, to emerge.

The tree waits patiently while the process of decay continues. The seed likewise remains covered with earth as growth progresses. We, too, need only to trust that God is causing our old self to decay as he brings about new life through all the circumstances He allows to take place as we live our lives.

If we stop looking for results, we're less likely to hamper the work of the Spirit. The more we forget about ourselves, the less inclined we will be to grow conceited or discouraged. No matter how far the Lord has brought us along the path of transformation, we must remember that we have an even greater distance to travel before we reach perfection. Only by letting God's love flower unobserved within ourselves and within each other will God be glorified and we be humbled.

In book 2, chapter 11 of <u>The Ascent of Mount Carmel</u> the, author St. John of the Cross urges us to even let go of all consolations in order to come into union with God.

O Lord, I Know You Are Near

"O LORD, I KNOW you are near" is the opening line of what I would refer to as a "reminder" hymn. I know this hymn is familiar, but permit me to recall the refrain for you:

> *"O Lord, I know you are near*
> *Standing always at my side.*
> *You guard me from the foe*
> *And you lead me in ways everlasting."*
> —Written by Dan Schutte

Although I find it hard to comprehend how God can be with everyone simultaneously, I do believe it is true. My mind is just too small to be able to grasp such a profound and all-encompassing presence. Whenever I find myself faced with this kind of incomprehensibility regarding God, I simply accept the fact as true and act on it. In that way, my mind resists the temptation to doubt and to be led into fear.

The song says that the Lord is "standing at my side". That image gives me a feeling that God is ready to do just as the next line suggests, "to guard me from the foe and to lead me …"

Sometimes I prefer to think of God as Father, or Jesus as friend, sitting beside me as they listen intently to what I am saying or as they watch what I am doing. But then, there are times when I think of God as creator or as a compassionate judge. As one who yearns for my love. One who is present in every situation, doing what He can to reach my heart, especially at those times when my heart has been hardened against Him.

Another favorite hymn that also reminds me of God's presence is "Be Not Afraid" by John Michael Talbot.

"Be not afraid
I go before you always.
Come follow me
And I will give you rest."

Here the image of God leading me helps me remember that if I follow behind Jesus, the Good Shepherd, I certainly have nothing to fear. The verses that follow describe precarious situations in which God promises to be present: in a barren desert, through raging waters, in the midst of burning flames and before the power of hell. If I am asked to trust God in these kinds of situations, how much more ought I to trust He will help me each day to face any and all trials and difficulties which come my way.

Other hymns invite me to "Taste and See (the Goodness of the Lord)" from Psalm 34:8 and to know that "Surely the Presence of the Lord Is in This Place" (by Lanny Wolfe). Then there's Brother Lawrence's book Practice the Presence of God, which asks us to do just that. I thank humble monk Brother Lawrence for writing this wise little book and the songwriters who grasped all these biblical truths and put them to music.

As I respond to these invitations to trust and wait on the Lord, I've found that God does stand beside me, that He does sit by me, and that He does go before me always. I have found that God is good and that He really is with me always.

On Being Hoodwinked

ONE HOT SUMMER DAY I made a perfectly sound decision to go river tubing the next week. But I didn't end up going because I was hoodwinked by the devil and by my lack of trust in God.

Do you know what hoodwinked means? Well, I do now. It means that a perfectly good decision gets changed because of faulty discernment and giving into fear and worry. The dictionary says it means "to deceive by false appearance." Or perhaps to deceive by lies, and who is the biggest liar? It's the devil himself who masquerades as wisdom by instilling fear and worry. Thus we turn away from performing some holy act or refrain from taking and enjoying some perfectly ordinary action or activity. We believe these lies. We act or refuse to act and end up tied in the knots of fear and worry.

God is a God of Peace. He never puts the fear of doing good deeds in our minds. Instead, He guides us in a peaceful way. As we move toward the objective with a trustful attitude, we will experience peace even though the devil will continue to hound us with fear and worry. How many times do we fall into this trap each day? Don't get hoodwinked by his lies!

This time my thoughts were predicated on concern for self. The weather had been oppressively hot and humid for weeks and weeks. It sapped my strength and put the fear of heat stroke in my mind. Since my skin is becoming thinner and drier because of aging, I feared further damage from four hours of exposure to the sun reflecting off the water. I also didn't consult anyone, including my husband, for his opinion. I became totally suckered into the deception. I should have known better, but I didn't act wisely or prudently.

Result: I spent a very rainy day at home. It rained for hours. I was sad and lonely and not at peace. When I checked the weather where the tubing was taking place, I found that the temperature was moderate and the sky was partly cloudy. It was an ideal day for tubing ___so much for not discerning correctly.

How many times have I been hoodwinked by worry and fear? How many times have I not corrected a loved one when I noticed that they were taking an unwise or sinful path? How many graces have I lost in this manner, and how many loved ones were not turned away from evil or stupidity because I gave into the temptation to allow myself to be hoodwinked by the fear of rejection?

Please, dear Lord, save me from myself.

One Resolution: Two Approaches

The Do It Yourself Approach

Dear Lord,

I really want to stop smoking. Smoking is expensive and bad for my health. Someone told me of a good method to use to break the habit.

I must really want to quit.

I need to break the routine that leads to the habit.

I should substitute some other form of behavior.

I must announce my resolution to others and ask them to reinforce me by complimenting me on my successes and not mention my times of failure.

When I have finally broken this habit I will feel proud, happy, and self-satisfied. I know it's going to be agonizing, but I'll grit my teeth and get through somehow. After all, I have great willpower.

Love, Mike

Dear Son,

You have acknowledged your need to give up the habit of smoking. That is a good and noble desire. Your method is very sound, humanly speaking, and your friends will certainly praise you for your success. I wish you well.

Love, Jesus

The "Without Me You Can Do Nothing" Approach

Dear Lord,

You have taught me to ask you to reveal to me anything in my life that displeases you and is a barrier between us. I have asked and you have indicated to me that you want me to stop smoking. You are right, I am addicted to nicotine. Jesus, you said, "Without me you can do nothing," and "I have come to bring you new life. I have come to set the captives free. My grace is sufficient for you."

I believe this is true, and I trust in your power to deliver me from this addiction to nicotine. I humbly submit myself to you and acknowledge my weakness before the Christian community. I ask them for their prayerful intercession May You alone be glorified.

Love, John

Dear Son,

You have heard my desire for you to stop smoking and you recognize the true source of the power over evil, sin, and weakness. Because I am a loving Father I delight in giving good gifts to my children when they ask for them. You have asked and trusted and abandoned yourself into My hands. Therefore, I will send forth my Spirit to recreate you in this area of your life and set you free. As you proclaim the great work I have done for you, I will be glorified and praised.

Love, Jesus

One Thing Leads To Another

Self knowledge leads to wisdom
Wisdom to repentance
Repentance to reconciliation
Reconciliation to holiness, love, joy
and peace.
Stubbornness leads to stalemate
Stalemate to anger
Anger to illness
Illness to inability to function
Inability to function to division
Division to hatred
Hatred to death of a relationship
So come, let us reason together.
Let us come to truly know ourselves
Let us face our realities
Let us seek repentance
Let us open our lives to healing
and reconciliation
Let us come to love each other again.

Not A Victimless Crime

WHILE WE CONTINUE THE senseless debate on the rights of individuals to buy or distribute pornographic material, thousands of women and children become victims of the industry. Pornographic "trash" can be found not only in our cities but in small towns, rural areas, and in our homes.

Covenant House knows firsthand what the faces and experiences of the victims of the racket look like. Covenant House is a privately-run shelter that provides a haven for homeless kids who get caught up in the world of pimps, prostitution, and pornography. Some are as young as eleven-year-old Veronica, who was ultimately thrown out of a tenth-story window and killed by a customer or her pimp.

Every year the staff cares for more than twenty thousand kids who have become victims of the sex industry and come seeking temporary help or a permanent way out. Each night the staff combs the streets of the city, risking their lives as they reach out to offer these kids a lifeline. Because of the violent nature of the racket and the people involved, the street kids risk their lives when they do "grasp the hand" of Covenant House volunteers.

Pornography is far from an innocent, victimless, individual act, and moral outrage isn't enough. All of society becomes a victim of this heinous crime.

So what can be done? Where do we start?

How about starting at home by providing warm, loving, intact families: fathers who respect their wives and children; parents with authentic religious values who respect themselves and teach their children what it means to be a child of a loving God; and men and women whose goals reach out for something more than materialism and the gratification of their lust or the desire for power over others.

The volunteers at Covenant House and all the other outreach organizations who are on the streets rescuing our children ask us to pray for courage; to plead for courage to criticize; courage to be considered book burners and fanatics; courage to take moral positions; and courage even to lose friends. As long as we keep silent, pornography and prostitution will continue to flourish. Speak out! Support the organizations that act on their conviction that pornography is a deadly crime and reach out to give a hand to a child caught in this web of evil—and pray, pray, pray!

Praying Scripture A Key To Holiness

PRAYER IS MORE THAN something we do. Rather, it's a relationship we enter into with the one who alone can bring us into holiness, and Scripture is an essential part of this relationship. Through the prayerful reading of God's Word and with the aid of the Holy Spirit, we are able to hear God speak to our minds and hearts.

In 2 Timothy 3:16–17 Paul says that **"all scripture is inspired by God and is useful for teaching, for refutation, for correction, and for training in righteousness, so that one who belongs to God may be competent and equipped for every good work."**

Like the potter's clay, we need to be pliable in God's hands. It's through humble prayerful reading of Scripture that we place ourselves daily in the Creator's hands. We invite Him to speak to our hearts, to mold us, and to shape us into more perfect, holy vessels. It's in and through prayer that we yield to the work of the Holy Spirit.

In the prayerful reading of Scripture, we come to recognize God's voice as He speaks to us. Scripture is like a window through which we glimpse the God who made us. Scripture is also like a mirror as it accurately reflects who we truly are and shows us where we need transformation.

In James 1:21–22, we are instructed to **"put away all filth and evil excess and humbly welcome the word that has been planted in you and is able to save your souls. Therefore, we are admonished to "be doers of the word and not hearers only, deluding yourselves."** That's like building a house upon sand rather than on a rock foundation.

Prayer without relationship is empty. Prayer without humility is bound to fail. Prayer without action lies dormant and unproductive.

However, by absorbing God's Word, the source of all wisdom and power, by yielding to the hand's of the Potter in a loving relationship and by obeying God's commandments and putting His Word into action, we can and will grow in holiness through God's love and grace. Then to God we can give the glory.

Private Litany For Humility

From the desire of being praised
From the desire of being honored
From the desire of being preferred
From the desire of being consulted
From the desire of being approved
From the desire of comfort and ease
From the fear of being humiliated
Jesus, deliver me.
From the fear of being criticized
From the fear of being passed over
From the fear of being lonely
From the fear of being hurt
From the fear of suffering
Jesus, deliver me.
That others may be loved more than I.
Jesus, grant me the grace to desire it.
That others may be chosen and I set aside.
Jesus, grant me the grace to desire it.
That others may be praised and I unnoticed.
Jesus, grant me the grace to desire it.
"Jesus, meek and humble of heart, make my heart like unto
Thine".

Take Time To Ponder #4

IT IS MOST BENEFICIAL if your reflections are written down and pondered often.

- Do I pray first for the person I am concerned about to be open to the grace of God, the promptings of the Holy Spirit, and to have a change of heart?
- First we need to repent. Have I repented? Has the person I'm praying for repented and believes in Jesus?
- I have prayed persistently and yet no answer has come. Do I accept the silence, say thanks, and trust that all will be well? Read Habakkuk 3:15–19.
- Do I trust in God's goodness and His love for me even when I am living in the valley of darkness?
- How does my faith compare to the faith of these ancient believers? Meditate on Hebrews 11.
- Do I realize that everyone suffers, even the people we don't know, because of my sins and the sins of others?
- What is my image of God? How did I form this image? Is it the correct image or should I look into the matter through Scripture and the teaching of the Catholic Church?
- Who or what is my God? Upon who, what, or where do I spend most of my time and energy?
- With suffering comes the grace to endure it, but only if we trust. Do I believe this?
- Do I remember to invite the Saints or other prayerful people to join in my prayer for either myself or someone else?

Reaching Out

Let's pray for those

- who believe;
- who practice their faith but are lukewarm;
- who believe but don't practice their faith;
- who have abandoned God;
- who have authority over others;
- who live in broken relationships marriages, families, friendships, citizens, countries, and parishes;
- who are victims of natural disasters, crime, war, accidents, hatred, prejudice, and separation;
- who are addicted to drugs, alcohol, tobacco, pornography, other substances, and evil acts;
- who are sick spiritually, mentally, physically, or emotionally;
- who are abandoned, abused, poor, unemployed, homeless, hungry, cold, lonely, or afraid;
- who perpetuate injustices;
- who lead others into sin through pornography, drugs, prostitution, abortion, or bad example;
- who are dying;
- who have died;
- who are missionaries;
- who are serving in battle somewhere in the world;
- who are celebrating birthdays, anniversaries, or other special occasions;
- who have special needs or desires;
- who are making crucial decisions;
- who seek to know, love, and serve God better;

- who seek to grow and to be delivered from all that is displeasing to God; and
- who are called to religious life, marriage or the single state.

May all these circumstances and these souls be touched by God's Grace.

Reluctant Samaritan

ONE SUNDAY MORNING AFTER his homily, our parish priest asked the congregation if one of us would please volunteer to visit an elderly homebound parishioner. I heard the call but rationalized that I was not the one who should respond. After all, hadn't I just resigned from a host of committees in order to get my life in order? Besides that, I certainly didn't want to get tied to any long-term commitment.

The following Sunday, Father asked again. This time my conscience urged me to offer to find someone to visit her. Unfortunately, everyone I asked gave the same sick excuses I had used.

That did it! This time the Lord came through loud and clear, like the recruitment poster—THE US ARMY NEEDS YOU—finger pointing and all.

On my first visit, a handicapped, eighty-four-year-old woman greeted me like a long lost friend. She lived in a small pink trailer with her parakeet and a tiny goldfish, her only true friends. I felt a tug on my heart strings as she poured out her story. The list of physical, psychological, and emotional, complaints were numerous. The saddest of all were the many broken relationships and hurts of the past. Fortunately, she was open to the healing power of God and eager to work with His grace.

Week after week we asked the Lord to heal and deliver her from all the hurts of the past and the present. She asked forgiveness for any pain she had inflicted that had caused others to turn away from her. Gradually, over a period of two years, Jesus' peace, His joy, and His love began to be ever-present in her life.

It wasn't long before she became a co-disciple; praying for and ministering to her neighbors who came as friends and as people in need and to her family members. I continued to visit my friend each week for a period of eight years. She died reconciled to her daughter, her son-in-law, and her granddaughter, all of whom the Lord had slowly but surely healed and transformed.

As we prayed together in person and on the phone over those many years, I watched in awe as God's grace and healing power worked. The Lord also blessed me as He blessed my friend and her family.

To this day, however, I know that had I not understood and been taught how to pray for healing and deliverance through the Charismatic Renewal, I would merely have listened compassionately and offered only some popular psychological advice. Instead, the Lord taught me how to use the most powerful gift with which He desires to endow those who are open and receptive.

That gift is to pray in the power and in the name of Jesus through the indwelling of the Holy Spirit. May all Christians discover the power of repentance and the power of this special healing prayer so God can work through us to heal and deliver one another. To God give the glory for the things He can and wants to do.

Scripture Meditations

Divine Love:

- Treatise on Divine love I John 1–5
- The true vine and the hostile world John 15:1–27
- The greatest commandment Mark 12:28–34
- Love of God Deuteronomy 6:4
- Love of neighbor Leviticus 19:9–18
- Love of enemy Matthew 5:43–48
- Unity preserved in humility Philippians 2:1–11

Trust In God:

- Trust in God John 14:1
- Call on God for help Psalm 51
- Trust God and not the world or self Matthew 6:32–34
- Purpose of prophecy1 Corinthians 14:3

Prayer:

- Be alone to pray Luke 5:15
- How to pray Matthew 6:7–15
- Two ways to pray I Corinthians 13:15
- The Holy Spirit expresses our plea Romans 8:26
- Cry to the Lord Lamentations 2:18–19
- Persevere in prayer Ephesians 6:18–20
- Transformation through prayer 2 Corinthians 3:18

Suffering Needed:

- Renunciation necessary Luke 14:25–33
- Take up your cross Matthew 16:24–26

- Lose your life Mark 8:34–38
- Throw off what hinders you Hebrews 12:1–4
- Suffering a part of training Hebrews 12:5–13
- Be prepared to suffer 1 Peter 4:1-6
- Learn obedience through suffering Hebrews 5:7
- Only the Lord satisfies Isaiah 55:1–3
- Life of an apostle I Corinthians 4:9–13

False Prophets And Teachers:

- Beware of false prophets and teachers 2 Timothy 4:1–5
- False prophets are slaves to Satan Revelations 13:11–18
- Proclaim Jesus' resurrection Acts 17:16-34
- False wisdom versus true wisdom I Corinthians 1:17-31,2:1-16, 3:18-20

Spiritual Warfare:

- Powers of darkness Ephesians 6:10–13
- Evil spirits cast down to earth Revelations 12:1–17
- Worshiping false gods Exodus 20:1–7
- Detestable practices Deuteronomy 18:9–12
- Be on guard—test the spirits I John 4:1–6
- Deliverance Mark 5:1–20
- Infilling of the Holy Spirit needed Matthew 12:43–45
- New creation and punishment Revelations 21:1–8
- Time is close Revelations 22:10–15

Set Free!

THE WEIGHT OF SIN oppresses us and robs us of our freedom. It destroys our relationship with ourselves, our fellow man, and with God. One of God's greatest gifts to us is the gift of forgiveness of sin, and as members of Christ's Mystical Body, the Church, we are especially blessed with the Sacrament of Reconciliation (Penance).

There is nothing more joyful than being freed from sin. The hardest part is to admit one is a sinner and then to pray for the courage to do something about it. Like others, I find it difficult to walk into the confessional, but walking out is glorious. The bigger the sin the greater the joy received.

Going in is like facing an icy, winter wind, and coming out is like experiencing the first day of warm weather. It is like taking a final exam and afterward knowing you've earned an A. It is like being ill and suddenly being well. Acknowledging and confessing our sins is worth the agony because the peace, joy, and freedom we experience after confession reaches the very core of our being and sets us free.

In the sacrament of Reconciliation we come to know the love of Jesus Christ. He has promised:

"Come to me, all you who labor and are burdened, and I will give you rest"—Matthew 11:28.

"Learn to savor how good the Lord is; happy are those who take refuge in him"—Psalm 34:9.

"For freedom Christ set us free; so stand firm and do not submit again to the yoke of slavery"—Galatians 5:1.

What a priceless gift! Cherish reconciliation.

Sharing Our Treasures

ALL THE TALENTS AND spiritual gifts we enjoy are from God. They need to be developed and used for His greater honor and glory; they need to be used in order to bring others to a fuller knowledge and love of our Heavenly Father. People's individual talents and gifts are a reflection of God as we experience Him in time and space. That is, we sense God's presence as these talents and gifts are shared in Jesus' name through the power of the Holy Spirit. They are God's Graces, which flow into all creation touching hearts and healing souls.

In 1 Corinthians 12:4–11, Paul says there are **"different kinds of spiritual gifts but the same Spirit … the expression of wisdom … the expression of knowledge … faith … gifts of healing … mighty deeds … prophecy … discernment of spirits … various tongues … interpretation of tongues."**

In 1 Corinthians 12: 27–31, Paul says that as members of the Body of Christ we are first Apostles; second, prophets; third, teachers; then, mighty deeds; then gifts of healing, assistance, administration, and varieties of tongues.

Let us ask God to help us discern and use the gifts He has given each of us for the building up of the Body of Christ, the Church. Also, let us seek to find our place in the Body of Christ so we can exercise the gifts properly. The laity is invited and expected to do more than pray, pay and obey. We all are called to be a blessing, not a burden, to our brothers and sisters in Christ.

Sing Praise

"Sing to the mountain
Sing to the sea.
Raise your voices, lift your hearts.
This is the day the Lord has made,
Let all the earth rejoice."
—Bob Dufford

DID YOU KNOW GOD truly inhabits the praises of His people? Have you ever tried to find God by singing praises to Him?

Have you ever participated in the songs of a group of people who love God and sing joyful songs of praise and worship?

Did you know that praise opens our hearts so that when we listen carefully as Scripture is read, prophecy is proclaimed, and prayers of love are offered, our hearts are warmed and we can hear and understand God's love.

The dictionary says that "praise" means to commend applause, to express approval or admiration, to extol, to glorify, etc.

A similar expression, "Give glory to God" means we acknowledge God for who He is and we confess and proclaim His Divinity with our words and our lives: we bless, praise, magnify, exult, and thank Him for His love, mercy, goodness, compassion, salvation, forgiveness, and a thousand other attributes too numerous to mention.

Psalm 95:1–3, 6–7 says, "**Come, let us sing joyfully to the Lord; cry out to the rock of our salvation. Let us greet him with a song of praise, joyfully sing out our psalms. For the Lord is a great God. … Enter, let us bow down in worship; let us kneel before the Lord who made us. For this is our God, whose people we are, and God's well-tended flock.**"

Search the Scriptures, especially the psalms, for reasons to praise God. Then, search through hymnals and Charismatic song books for songs of praise and worship to help you begin.

Those who sing praise reap countless blessings! So let praise be on our lips.

"Snack Pack" Of Thoughts

A Bright Idea

WHERE DID IT COME from? How should I respond? Who gets the credit? Here is some advice to consider:

When we receive a prompting to do something virtuous, we must ask ourselves: Is this prompting from God? Who will get the credit for this great idea? Is it a selfless act from which I derive no benefit? If I do what is asked, will the results glorify God alone? Will I remember to quietly thank God and praise only Him for the results?

Talents

God created us as we are. Therefore, we need to accept ourselves with both our talents and the lack of talents and use what we have been given for the Glory of God alone. We are called to do God's work where we are and with whom we are. We are to use all we have been entrusted with to bring about good for everyone. However, if we bask in our own self-righteousness, in our talents, and in the results that have been achieved, then all the good we have done will be destroyed and we will fall into the sin of pride. When possible, do all your good deeds in secret. Then your Father in Heaven will reward you.

Liberation

God created us in freedom, so when we freely submit to Him He can liberate us. Submission to God enables us to flow in the "river" of God's love and in His Divine Will. This alone will bring us fulfillment.

Listen Closely

Jesus is present among us in one another and in all that surrounds us. He comes to us in the ordinary and extraordinary happenings of our daily lives. He speaks to us as we listen to others. He serves us when we serve others. Grace opens our hearts and makes it possible for us to hear. Grace opens our eyes and makes it possible for us to see God at work in a variety of ways. If we don't invite God's grace to work in us, we will miss Him as He speaks to us continually during each day.

Put Yourself There

Put yourself into Scripture. Become part of the parables and episodes of Jesus' life and teachings. One by one take the place of each person present in the narrative. Ask yourself, "How would I feel about what's happening in this episode? How would I respond in this situation? How would I identify with the person to whom Christ is speaking? What is the Lord saying to me?" Let Scripture come alive in and for you.

Statements And Questions

THE ANCIENT MARINER CRIED, "Water, water everywhere, but not a drop to drink" Today's poor cry, "Money, money everywhere, but none to meet our needs."

In daily decision-making, like the mariner and the poor, I too wrestle with thought-provoking statements and questions (see below). Unless I resolve each statement or question through prayer, according to the mind of Christ, I find I have more questions than answers. Unless I take each situation on its own merits and apply proper, prayerful discernment, I won't know how to react. It takes courage to seek God's Will and to act on it. Lord, give me courage!

Take the following statements and questions one at a time and carefully consider each one. Which statements are the ones which should guide our decisions and which ones are the ones which lead us astray? Read the questions, and in each situation pray for the answers. Which are true? Which are false?

Starting Statements

Live according to your state in life.
Progress is our most important product.
Rich nations must satisfy the needs of poor nations.
The rich get richer and the poor get poorer.
Divide and conquer.
To the victor go the spoils.
Gluttony and self-indulgence, or sacrifice and sharing. It's my choice.
He who works gets. He who doesn't starves.
Set a little aside for a rainy day.
Be prudent and use God's gifts wisely.

Be a good steward.

Waste not, want not.

A penny saved is a penny earned.

Money is the root of all evil.

Luxury items and services also create employment.

I worked hard, therefore I deserve it.

The Lord loves a cheerful giver.

Taste and see the goodness of the Lord.

I have come that you might have abundant life.

The widow gave out of her need. The rich man gave out his surplus.

If you have two coats, share one with a neighbor.

Give and it shall be given to you.

The Lord is never outdone in generosity.

Don't let your right hand know what your left hand is doing.

Out of the first fruits of your labor, pay a tithe.

Trust in God. He will provide.

Deny yourself, and you will be blessed.

The poor you will always have with you.

Critical Questions

Why do the rich get richer and the poor get poorer?

Who are the poor?

Why are they poor?

How could my small sacrifice possibly help them?

When does our want become our need?

When is enough, enough?

Do I need this or do I just want it?

Just how many or how much of anything do I really need?

When is a simple lifestyle a better lifestyle?

How does conspicuous consumption begin?

Is conspicuous consumption always a sin?

Can it be a blessing?

Do I throw my money away on things that never satisfy?

What shall I do with my tithe?

What did Jesus mean when he promised us abundant life?

What motivates my spending habits?

Where does my obligation to the less fortunate begin?

Who is my neighbor?

When I buy goods and services, aren't I creating jobs?

When I demand more goods than I need, aren't I depleting the earth's resources?

How can the earth's resources be distributed more equitably?

How do I know when my spending habits are out of line?

If I give to the poor, won't they also be able to contribute to society?

Isn't it okay to have a consumer society that creates jobs through production?

How can I directly influence the life of an unemployed person?

When does giving help, and when does giving rob another of dignity?

Am I always my brother's keeper?

The Sacred Gift

SEXUAL INTERCOURSE IS SACRED and was ordained by God to be enjoyed by husbands and wives to express their committed love and fidelity for one another and to beget children. Through the sexual act married couples become co-creators with God in bringing forth new life. When used unselfishly, it is a most sacred expression of love and a source of grace to the married couple. It is a holy act.

Outside marriage, however, premarital and extramarital sexual intercourse as well as same sex acts are far from what God ordained it to be. It is unholy, unhealthy, and irresponsible. Its name is sin.

When society considers sex as a mere biological urge to be satisfied, and it denies its moral, spiritual, psychological, and physical ramifications, we open for ourselves and for society a Pandora's Box. By promoting condoms and other birth control devices, we imply our approval of irresponsible sexual acts. Instead, why not pass out the word of truth about the sanctity of sex and the effect illicit sexual acts have on the individual and society?

Each year throughout the world, billions and billions of dollars are spent glorifying irresponsible and valueless sexual relationships through every form of entertainment and advertising. Efforts to promote holy and healthy attitudes about the sexual act are called puritanical and an interference in our rights and freedoms.

One of the best ways to discern if an act is sinful or not is to look at the consequences of the action. For instance, look at the evils that have been thrust upon society: recall to mind the deadly AIDS epidemic; the increased number of broken marriages, broken homes, and broken hearts; daily reports of child abuse; wholesale abortion; an increasing number of suicides and mental health problems; as well as an epidemic of drug and alcohol addictions that lead to theft and murder. It's not a pretty picture. It is said also that more than any other sin; illicit sexual acts lead the participants away from God, our loving Father, and into so-called agnosticism or denial of His existence. We have truly reaped what we have sown.

God entrusted us with the sacred gift of sexual intercourse. If we use this gift according to His plan, we will be blessed instead of cursed.

Thirsting

"O GOD, YOU ARE my God—for you I long! For you my body yearns; for you my soul thirsts, like a land parched, lifeless, and without water"—Psalm 63.

Whenever I read this psalm, these words echo in my memory for hours. One day my thoughts dwelt not only on my own thirst but on the object of my thirst. I began thinking about our God, who thirsts to excess. Our God thirsted for each of us to His death. It's hard to comprehend such a loving thirst, isn't it? Jesus suffered unbearable torture before He died. But both then and now His greatest and most lasting suffering was and is His desire to be loved by us in return.

To get some inkling of this love that God has for us, His children:

- Consider how we feel when we are rejected by a friend, a spouse, or a child.
- Consider how we feel when no one responds to our needs, our ideas, or our love.
- Consider how we feel when our spouse turns a cold shoulder when we're in need of understanding and affection.
- Consider how we feel when our children ridicule us and refuse to obey our wise counsel.
- Consider how we feel when our friends abandon us because we're sick or aged or they just can't be bothered.

Don't these situations cause us to feel hurt, and don't they leave us with a feeling of emptiness and loneliness?

Now let's consider the countless opportunities Jesus offers us every moment of every day to experience His love His grace and His mercy and forgiveness. Do we return love for love?

- Consider how Jesus hungers to speak to us and to listen to us in prayer. Do we take time to have a conversation with Him?
- Consider how Jesus wrote love letters to us in what we call Scripture (the Bible). Do we read His love letters so we can draw closer to Him?
- Consider how His Saints have communicated his love through their writings. Do we take time to ponder their experiences?
- Consider how through His Church, He shows us how to live in order to be filled with peace and joy. Do we listen and obey out of love or do we listen to the world?
- Consider how He offers us His beloved Mother, Mary, to be our mother and our closest friend. Do we pay attention to her love and listen to her pleadings?
- Consider how He offers us countless graces through the Sacrament of Reconciliation. Do we take time to ask God to show us our true selves and to repent for what we find?
- Consider how He feeds us with the heavenly food of His Body, Blood, Soul, and Divinity in the most Holy Eucharist to strengthen us on our journey to eternity. Do we take advantage of all the Sunday and daily Masses offered each week, or do we drive by with barely a nod in His direction as He waits in the tabernacle as a prisoner out of love for us?

Who Or What Is the Center of Our Lives?

Are we lukewarm?

Are we indifferent?

In Revelations 3:15–16, God warns us, "**I know your works; I know that you are neither cold nor hot. I wish you were either cold** or hot. So, because you are lukewarm, neither hot nor cold, I will spit you out of my mouth."

Jesus yearns for souls to quench His thirst. His thirst is to be loved and appreciated.

In response, do we cry out, "Yes, Lord, my soul is thirsting for you, oh Lord my God. I love you, I praise you, I adore you, I bless you, and I thank you. Dear Jesus, I repent of my indifference, my cold heartedness and I beg your forgiveness."

To Acquire "It"

TO HAVE PEACE OF MIND,
MIND YOUR OWN LIFE!

Take Time To Ponder #5

IT'S MOST BENEFICIAL IF your reflections are written down and pondered often.

- Scripture says to pray and not lose heart. Do I follow this?
- Despair is the loss of hope—the deadliest of sins. Discouragement is the devil's strongest weapon. When my prayers aren't answered, do I give in to despair and discouragement?
- Have I ever used prayer and fasting, a healthy combination, as a gimmick to bargain with God? "I'll give up smoking if you find me a job?" Right? Wrong?
- When and how am I responsible for the salvation of another?
- What effect does my lack of faith have on others?
- What place does doubt play in unanswered prayer? Do I usually pray in doubt or with faith?
- How can I handle and encourage myself and others as I wait in sorrow for an answer that never seems to come?
- Does God seem to be waiting for me or another person to change before He can or will be able to act? First, should I ask Him what change He wants me to make with His help so He can act?

Treasure Rediscovered

UPON AWAKENING ONE MORNING I realized I was unconsciously reciting the prayers I had memorized as a child. I began to think about the words and phrases of these gems of my childhood and was surprised by their beauty and significance, their wisdom and sentiments. What a rich treasure of spirituality we've received and how fortunate it is that we committed these sacred words to memory. Now without any effort, it's possible to reach into our storehouse and speak to our God with these beautiful words, like countless others do and have done throughout the centuries.

Take a close look at the words and phrases of the following prayers:

Our Father; Hail Mary; Glory Be; Act of Contrition; Acts of Faith, Hope, and Charity; Apostles' Creed and Nicene Creed; Hail Holy Queen; Blessings before and after meals; prayers to St. Michael and our Guardian Angel.

Remember how they were part of growing up in the Faith? As an individual did you, like me, recite these prayers by merely rattling off the words with barely a thought as to what the words meant? Find a copy of each prayer and take a long, meditative look at the words. These words should create images in our minds. Images to be cherished, such as "Our Father."

Or how about "Hail Holy Queen," "Glory be to the Father," or "St. Michael, defend us in battle"? Each word, each phrase conjures up priceless images to be contemplated. A prayerful recitation of these prayers can reap countless blessings while giving glory to God and bringing Him joy. It's a win-win situation.

Perhaps, like me, you too have overlooked or set aside this enduring treasure. Sometimes it happens that as we grow in our relationship with God we naturally expand the forms of prayers we use. We add joyful songs, conversational and contemplative prayer, meditation on Scripture, praying in the Spirit, the Jesus prayer, praying in the Divine Will, etc.

However, since I've rediscovered the power of these rote or formal prayers, I have reincorporated them into my daily prayer life without sacrificing the newer forms of prayer. Together they have enhanced my relationship with God. Now, instead of rattling them off as I did as a child, I've enjoyed spending time allowing the words to penetrate my mind, my heart and my soul until they open my life to the transforming power of God's grace.

In addition to private, personal prayer, rediscover the power these rote prayers have when recited together in a slow, thoughtful manner. Discover how they can unite us in body, mind, soul, and spirit. Experience how they draw us into a single voice worshiping, praising, and petitioning the Trinity and the heavenly court. Notice how, when prayed in unison, it's like a choir of angels singing, but when prayed carelessly it becomes a discordant distraction.

Therefore, whether prayed alone or together, let the thoughtful recitation of rote prayers anoint us in love.

Universal Corruption

"Roam the streets of Jerusalem,
Look about and observe,
Search through her public places,
To find even one
Who lives uprightly and seeks to be faithful,
And I will pardon her!"—*Jeremiah 5:1*

NO MATTER WHAT THE Lord permitted to befall them, they refused to be corrected and they grew even harder of heart and wouldn't turn to the Lord. Both the lowly and the great refused to follow God. No wonder they had trouble.

The people have forsaken God, they swear by false gods, and they commit adultery by loving someone or something more than God. Shouldn't God take vengeance on them and punish them? After all, they have rebelled against Him. They no longer belong to Him. Shouldn't He ravish them for their open rebellion? They don't think anything will happen to them. The words of the prophet have been forgotten. Their own sinfulness will destroy them.

The words the Lord gives to Jeremiah are like fire and will consume the people like fire consumes wood. A nation they neither know nor understand will come against them, devouring their harvest, bread, sons, daughters, sheep, cattle, vines, fig trees, and the entire city. God will do these things because people have forsaken Him to serve strange gods. They will now be sent to serve strangers in a land not their own. (The Babylonian captivity was one of these incidents.)

Senseless and foolish people who can neither see nor hear because of their stubborn and rebellious hearts should fear the Lord. He is the one who made the sandy shore the limit of the sea, and no matter

121

how much the sea rages it cannot pass. You must fear the Lord. He is the one who gives the rain and watches over the appointed weeks of the harvest.

It is their own sins that have turned back the blessing from them. There are criminals among my people and houses full of treachery. My people grow powerful and rich, fat and sleek. Instead of defending justice for the fatherless and the poor, they go their own way. On a nation such as this, shall I not take vengeance?

Something shocking and horrible has happened in the land. The prophets prophecy falsely, and the priests teach as they wish. The people are satisfied with the way things are going. But what will happen when the end comes? ___Jeremiah 5:1–31 paraphrased.

See the parallel of Jerusalem's indiscretions to the situation in the world today. Yet despite how evil we've become, God is willing to forgive. He seeks to find just one person who lives an upright life and who seeks to be faithful. God our Father is that loving and forgiving. We must not delay in seeking His forgiveness, or we will all surely perish.

Unwanted?

Unwanted. Who's unwanted? The unborn baby or the pregnancy?

Unwanted. Who's unwanted? The six million Jews Hitler decided were unwanted?

Unwanted. Who's unwanted? Our parents when they become too infirm to care for themselves and inconvenience us?

Unwanted. Who's unwanted? A crippled child or an emotionally disturbed teenager?

Unwanted. Who's unwanted? The prostitute, the criminal, the delinquent or any one of us sinners?

Unwanted. Who's unwanted? The other person who doesn't meet our qualifications—or you, who don't meet mine?

WHO'S TO DECIDE?

Unless we respect the right to life of the unborn, we will have no alternative than to lose respect for life in any form or at any stage.

To God, all life is precious and meaningful and loved by Him. Who has the God-given right to "choose" to destroy what God has created?

Who is qualified to "play God?"

Think about the little child:

Never to touch.

Never to see.

Never to experience.

Because someone chose to say this little child doesn't "belong."

Vulnerable?

THIS MORNING I WOKE up angry—angry at myself and angry at people in general. What is the latest scandal that mesmerizes us? Who are the public sinners who scandalize us, and rightly so? Who do we point fingers at, snicker at, and make self-righteous statements about in disgust?

But what about us, we little folk whose indiscretions tear at the very fiber of our being, destroying families and friendships in its wake? How in the world do we get ourselves into these compromising situations? What causes us to wake up one day and find that we too are caught in a web of destructive behavior that has broken our relationships, our homes, and ourselves in body, mind, soul, and spirit?

The answer is: we've been overcome by temptation.

We're in a world filled with people who lust after the things of the flesh. We've lost our God-centeredness, and we're trying to find happiness by filling our lives with things of all kinds that distract us from the source of all happiness. We've been told that God is dead and that He has no place in our lives. So in order to be fruitful and happy we look for guidance elsewhere. That proves to be a deadly trap of futility.

Consider these thoughts:

- Everyone is tempted daily to do what is evil to one degree or another.
- If we don't turn away from temptation immediately, we will most likely find ourselves succumbing to it.
- At first, temptations are small and almost insignificant. Then as we give into the little ones, those which follow will become more and more significant.

- Then, as we depend only on our own strength to combat the temptation we reap failure.
- When we toy with evil we get caught in its snare.
- If we are holy enough or fool enough to think we can resist and we enter into a situation where temptation abounds, we are asking for trouble.

Take a look at some seemingly innocent temptations that most of us face each day:

- Why not just turn off the alarm and go back to sleep for a few minutes?
- I can be a little late for work or be lazy and call in sick.
- I can run a red light or a stop sign to make up for lost time.
- It won't hurt to take an extra few minutes for a coffee break so I can gossip a bit longer.
- Don't worry about mistakes, just blame someone else.
- Get angry at some innocent stranger because something is bugging you.
- Lie to your children or spouse or boss rather than admit you are wrong.
- Spend more time with television or selfish pursuits and ignore the rest of your obligations.
- Have another drink or take a pill to get you through a situation.
- Don't pray; after all, who has time to waste time talking to yourself?
- Keep really busy so you don't have time to face the "real" you.
- Eat more than your body requires—and, of course, who needs exercise?
- Read something or watch some sexually stimulating or suggestive program to add a bit of excitement to your otherwise dull and uneventful life.

- Don't do anything to help someone less fortunate; aren't they just lazy, stupid people asking for a handout?
- Leave your spouse and find someone more to your liking.

The list could go on and on, day after day, week after week, month after month, and year after year until we are mesmerized into immobility against temptations as we watch ourselves fall deeper and deeper into habitual sin.

"Society" tells us we are self-sufficient and capable of resisting sin by exercising our willpower. It also tells us daily, ad nauseam, that we can't be happy unless we have or do this or that. But is that really so? Do we really need to satisfy all the desires, lusts, and passions of our hearts? Is that what leads to happiness, to fulfillment? Or do we find that the more we try to satisfy the desires of our flesh the more bankrupt we become?

The sexual sin that is running rampant throughout society is a prime example of our inability to resist temptation. In James 1:14–15 we are reminded that **"each person is tempted when he is lured and enticed by his own desire. Then desire conceives and brings forth sin, and when sin reaches maturity it gives birth to death."**

Human sexuality is one of God's greatest and most valuable gifts. That's why, like precious jewels, it's so vulnerable. Sexual intercourse is a priceless gift because it begets life and expresses committed love to one's spouse. When used wrongly, however, it begets "death."

Daily we are confronted with voices that tempt us to use our sexuality in inappropriate ways. The sources of temptations are numerous and varied: popular magazines, TV, plays, novels, videos, music, advertisements, friends, family members, neighbors, teachers, lawyers, movie makers, and so forth.

Sometimes it's blatant. Sometimes it's insidious. It erodes our resistance to guard and treasure this priceless gift. We willingly sacrifice ourselves to this brainwashing. When someone suggests this is dangerous and we ought not to subject ourselves to these temptations, we claim they're just being prudish. After all, we know right from wrong; our values are healthy. The next thing we know, we find we've sold out and bought the lie hook, line, and sinker.

In the past we were taught the following ways to deal with temptation and to avoid doing what was evil and sinful:

- Don't invite trouble by going to places or with people who are apt to lead you to sin.
- Don't read, look at, or dwell on things that are sexually arousing.
- When temptation comes, turn away immediately, leave the person or the situation, and pray for God's assistance.
- Rebuke the tempter by invoking the name of Jesus. Tell him to get lost.

In other words, most of the time we need to understand that we are the ones who let ourselves be led astray. To paraphrase a famous quotation: For what will it profit a person if he or she "has a little fun" but suffers the loss of his or her immortal soul?

God has given us a still, small voice within (a conscience) to guide us to inner peace and fulfillment. But how often do we listen instead to those other voices?

We live in a society that promises instant everything. Unfortunately, most instant things aren't that great. Some leave a nasty taste in our mouths. Others are totally empty, valueless "commodities." Whoever said that "life is easy" was sadly mistaken. Life is difficult. It's a challenge, but with God's help it's well worth the effort. The prize of right living is of inestimable value. It brings inner peace now and eternal life to follow. It produces healthy relationships, healthy bodies, minds, souls, and spirits and an abundant, challenging yet joy-filled life, here and for eternity.

In Deuteronomy 30:15–20, we hear God warning Israel against idolatry. He gives them a choice: choose His way or follow the way of the world. We are given this same choice: **"Hear, then, I have today set before you life and prosperity, death and doom"**—Deuteronomy

30:15. If we obey, we are promised blessings. If we disobey, we will perish.

In the Our Father, Jesus taught us to pray: "**do not subject us to the final test [temptation] but deliver us from the evil one.**" He warned us that the devil is the father of lies, and we soon see that gaining the whole world will cost us the loss of our immortal souls. We have been instructed by Jesus to take up our cross daily and follow in His footsteps. In other words, do it the hard way and reap a rich harvest. "**Blessed is the man who perseveres in temptation, for when he has been proved he will receive the crown of life that he promised to those who love him**"—James 1:12.

Why don't we wise up and recognize our own vulnerability? Let's stop pointing out the vulnerability of our fellow man and look at the vulnerability in our own lives. Let's pray for ourselves and for everyone, especially those public sinners we hear about. Then maybe they will pray for us. We need each other.

We Fall On Our Faces

EVERY TIME WE INSIST on doing anything ourselves, we invariably fall on our faces. Jesus warned us, **"Without Me you can do nothing"**—John 15:5. He also promised that He would be with us always, even to the end of time.

When we rely on God, nothing is impossible. Look at the incredible things the Saints accomplished. First they were obedient and faithful to the teachings and guidance of the Church, which Christ instituted to teach, govern, and sanctify the faithful. The Saints wisely and prayerfully listened to the promptings of the Holy Spirit within this context.

When a desire is implanted in our minds, do we turn to the Church, to the Scriptures, to wise, obedient, and prudent followers of Christ for advice? Or do we let the desire well up in us until it consumes our every thought and emotion until finally our passions are completely aroused and desire consumes us? Have we rationalized truth away until we have convinced ourselves that the "wrong way" is the only way?

God didn't ask us to figure out everything for ourselves. He didn't leave us orphans. Instead, He said, **"Turn to me, oh turn and be saved for I, the Lord, am God. There is no other, none beside Me. I call your name"**—Isaiah 45:22.

The Church is our mother, but she is also our sanctifier. She pours out grace upon us daily through the Mass and the Sacraments which nourish us on our way and give us courage and wisdom to do the right things and make the right decisions. We need only to ask, to listen, to trust, and to obey.

Look for peace of heart and mind. If we have chosen the right direction we will be at peace, and we will have eliminated the "middle step." We haven't fallen on our faces, and our acts will bear much fruit.

We're All In This Together

"MERCIFUL AND GRACIOUS IS the Lord, slow to anger, and abounding in kindness"—Psalm 103:8.

If our lives reflect these Christian virtues, people will use these words to describe us. When our lives radiate fairness, peacefulness, and gentleness we truly bring Christ to those around us. When we rejoice with those who rejoice and weep with those who weep, we mirror Christ's love and care.

Chapter one of the Book of Wisdom exhorts us to be just, for this is the key to life. Justice is the application of wisdom to moral conduct and is closely related to love and grace. Through justice, social inequities toward the disadvantaged are rectified, conditions that produce inequality are ended, oppressors are judged, and the oppressed are freed. Although justice is the responsibility of political authorities, we all play a significant role in obtaining justice and peace for all people.

Fulfillment of one's basic needs is the right of every man, woman, and child. When these rights and needs are violated or neglected, all of us in some way become enslaved and diminished. In contrast, regard for the rights and needs of the poor and the weak ultimately brings all of us into a right relationship within the community of man. Until justice becomes a reality, peace remains an impossibility.

What Is Like A Filthy Garage?

I STOOD IN FRONT of the open garage door with unbelieving eyes. The odor of mold and rotting food took my breath away. I instinctively stepped back. How in heaven's name had this handsome, two-car brick garage grown so unsightly!

Individual objects entangled and enmeshed with one another and had become indistinguishable. Broken chairs, castoff bed frames, and car seats sat abandoned; their beauty and usefulness had faded. A table saw was buried in a three inch mound of sawdust. Toys lay tangled with scraps of garbage. Tools, camping gear, paint, cassette tapes, and trash intertwined into a solid mass of chaos. Gnawed-opened garbage bags and filthy scraps of carpeting formed a foundation for this incredible array of discards.

The pile of debris rose nearly five feet, not including things piled on the shelves and the workbench. Believe it or not, however, in the dark recesses of these piles lay rare and priceless treasures.

Sometime in the midst of sorting, shoveling, tossing, disentangling, and hauling I began to see how a life of habitual sin, lack of virtue, bad habits, addictions, and refusal to forgive could transform one's inner self into a filthy garage.

Habitual sin, refusal to forgive, and those other bad characteristics resemble garbage bags of chaos dumped into the "garage of our being." Each day as we add to our soul bag after bag of this rotting, sinful chaos, we reflect not the loving God who created us but instead the garage of garbage described earlier.

Then in fear we close the garage door of ourselves so others can't detect our miserable inner-selves. Our God-given attributes lay buried under the dark, ugly pile of sin-bags. But day after day circumstances gnaw at the garage door behind which we hide and the stench of evil leaks out into our daily actions and attitudes. The stench permeates our façade and destroys our relationships.

Then we hate ourselves. We come to hate anyone we suspect sees the truth about us; we strike out; we become anti-social and self-destructive. These bad characteristics lead to physical, moral, mental, spiritual, and social debilitation.

But the Good News is, it doesn't have to be this way because Jesus is the greatest of all garage cleaners. He not only loves us in spite of the garbage we collect, He is willing and eager to help us shovel out our bags of sin, lack of forgiveness, weakness in virtue, bad habits, addictions, and our refusal to love Him.

If we sincerely ask for His help, Jesus promises to respond. That's what His death and resurrection are all about. That's what Savior means. Jesus came to save us from our miserable, sinful selves. He remakes us into the beautiful, gifted, loving persons God created us to be. Trust Him. He is most trustworthy!

However, if we refuse Jesus' help, we will continue to act out of the ugliness, the filth, the disorder, the waste, the hatred, and the envy of a sin-filled inner self. Our lives will continue to resemble a filthy garage The choice is ours.

Who Needs Them?

WHY DO CHRISTIANS THINK they need to turn to Oriental and Eastern religions or to New Age do-it-yourself techniques in order to gain peace and bolster their prayer life? I contend that Christians not only don't need this influence in their lives, but I believe these techniques are potentially dangerous to our union with Jesus, our Lord and Savior.

In John's Gospel, Thomas asked, "**Lord, we do not know where you are going. How can we know the way?**" Jesus said to him: "**I am the way and the truth and the life. No one comes to the Father except through Me.**"—John 14:5–6. Throughout the New Testament we are taught to pray in the name of Jesus. "**If you ask anything of me in my name, I will do it**"—John 14:14. Like the Apostles, we also need to ask Jesus how to pray. Jesus taught them the perfect form of prayer, the Our Father.

Jesus became man and died to set us free—to bring us New Life. Are we bothered by fear, frustrations, anxieties, sinful behavior, distress, and distractions? What is needed is "Some One," Jesus, not some thing, a technique. We don't need anything that distracts us and keeps us away from Jesus and our dependence on Him for everything. Christianity is not a do-it-yourself/save-yourself religion.

If we choose Jesus, we choose life and peace of soul. If we choose Satan or any of his multiple, deceitful distractions, empty promises, or sinful behaviors, we are bound to find ourselves living a life of turmoil, confusion, sin, and ultimately Hell.

Jesus promises to satisfy our deep yearning for love and peace. He invites those who are burdened by the cares of this world to come to Him and He will refresh us. Other traditions promise the same thing, but instead of drawing us to the source of New Life, they distract us from Jesus and substitute a counterfeit.

Why listen to teachers who don't know Jesus? Why not listen to the Son of God Himself as He teaches us through Scripture; through the Church He founded on Peter and the Apostles; through the Sacraments which feed us; through the teachings and the examples of the Saints; and through the inspired Christian teachers who have Jesus as the center of their teaching?

We don't need to be distracted by Oriental, Eastern, New Age, or any other pagan philosophies. Follow Christ, and He will give us the crown of everlasting life in Heaven. **"I am the Lord, there is no other; I form the light, and create the darkness, I make well-being and create woe; I the Lord, do all these things"**—Isaiah 45:7. **"It is I who made the earth and created mankind upon it"**—Isaiah 45:12.

Only Jesus can bring us new life without evil influence attached.

Who's In Charge?

HAVE YOU EVER SERIOUSLY asked yourself, Just who is in charge of my life? After even the briefest of soul searching, I am sure that most if not all of us would come to the realization that our relationship with Jesus falls far short of the true meaning of Lordship.

If Jesus is truly the Lord of my life, it means that I have given Him complete control over me and I praise Him for all that comes my way. I know that He cares for me even more than I care for myself.

Here is a brief list of some thought-provoking questions:

- Am I willing and eager to spend time and effort communicating with Jesus in prayer, even to the point of rising early or taking time during the day to withdraw from the hustle and bustle of life?
- Do I seek His Will in everything I do and in every relationship I have, or do I choose to ignore Him and just do whatever I want?
- When I ask Him for something, do I wait patiently and trust in His wisdom, or do I become impatient and take matters into my own hands?
- Do I really trust in His love and care for me and my loved ones?
- Am I joyful even when things are not going my way, and do I praise Him in all circumstances since I trust Him to bring good out of evil?
- Does Jesus come before all else or are there people, things and attitudes that are holding me in bondage?
- When I seek Jesus are my motives pure and am I willing to give Him everything I have? Remember, Jesus comes

to us only to the degree that we are willing to abandon all we are and all we have to Him.

- Do I recognize that I am a sinner and in need of God's mercy, love and forgiveness?

Based on my answers, I can begin to see just who is in charge.

Who's Speaking?

A DEEP PRAYER LIFE, an obedient spirit, a waiting, open heart, an ability to listen, and a spiritual companion are some of the requirements we need to fulfill before we can recognize God's voice and understand what He is calling us to do.

Like the desert hermits of the past and the contemplatives of the present, we must learn to withdraw into the quiet within ourselves, listen prayerfully, and wait patiently for the Spirit to speak to us in the depths of our being. He speaks through other people, circumstances, Scripture, authentic spiritual writers, and the teaching Church. God's voice is gentle, not demanding. It brings peace, not consternation. His requests and guidance never contradict Scripture or the official teachings of the Catholic Church and are based on love of God, neighbor, and self.

A life of prayer and proper discernment of the promptings of the Holy Spirit also requires the help of a spiritual companion. For without a guide we are more apt to flounder and fall into many pitfalls along the way. For there are countless voices calling to us: our own spirit, the evil spirit, the world's spirit, and the Holy Spirit.

Our spiritual companion helps us discern which spirit is speaking and what is being said. He or she also guides our self evaluation and encourages us to look at where we are, where we are going, and how each prompting helps or hinders our progress toward a deeper relationship with God.

Weekly, monthly, or periodic dialogues with our spiritual companion, obedience to God through obedience to those whom he has empowered to guide us and faithfulness to a Christian community who are experienced in God's ways will enable us to find the pathway to freedom and proper discernment. We are very adept at rationalization and often hear only what we choose to hear.

Our aim must always be to discover the true Christ and not the Christ we want Him to be.

Seek out a director or a spiritual companion by consulting others who have been helped. Look for someone who is open to the Holy Spirit, someone who recognizes the Spirit's movement within the Body of Christ, and someone who is wise, truthful, and prudent. Seek someone who is obedient to the official teachings of the Catholic Church, not someone who is at odds with it.

But most important, look for someone who leads a life of holiness and functions out of a deep, personal prayer life. The companion/director must also be under direction before attempting to help others discern God's voice. The effort is well worth the trouble if you are serious.

Why Should Christians Pray?

ARE YOU TIRED OF Christianity without effect on your problems or on the needs of our times? Have you ever read a book that really grabbed you? Well, that's how <u>Destined for the Throne</u> by Paul E. Billheimer affected me.

Although prayer has been the main focus of my life, Billheimer's book opened new Scriptural-based vistas. His underlying theme is the biblical fact that prayer is the work of the Church. Unless we pray, God cannot act. In order not to dilute Billheimer's thesis with commentary, permit me to quote from his introduction.

"The Church, by virtue of her faithful use of prayer, wields the balance of power not only in world affairs but also in the salvation of individual souls.

"Prayer is not begging God to do something He is loath to do. It is not overcoming reluctance in God. It is, instead, enforcing Christ's victory over Satan. It is implementing upon Earth Heaven's decisions concerning the affairs of men. Calvary legally destroyed Satan and canceled all of his claims. God placed the enforcement of Calvary's victory in the hands of the Church (Matt. 18:18 and Luke 10:17–19). He has given to the Church the 'power of attorney' … she is His deputy.

"But this delegated authority is wholly inoperative apart from the prayer of a believing church. Therefore, prayer is where the action is located. Any church without a well-organized and systematic prayer program is simply operating a religious treadmill.

"A program of prayer without faith is powerless. … The missing element that is necessary to energize triumphant faith is praise: perpetual, purposeful, aggressive praise. Praise is the highest form of prayer because it combines petition with faith. … It is the one thing needed to get faith airborne enabling it to soar above the deadly miasma of doubt. Praise is the detergent which purifies faith and purges doubt from the heart. The secret to answered prayer is faith without doubt (Mark 11:23). And the secret of faith without doubt is praise, triumphant praise, continuous praise, praise that is a way of life."

With Joyful Hearts

"COME, LET US SING joyfully to the Lord; cry out to the rock of our salvation. Let us greet him with a song of praise, joyfully sing out our psalms"... "Enter, let us bow down in worship; let us kneel before the Lord who made us. For this is our God, whose people we are, God's well-tended flock"—Psalm 95:1–2, 6–7.

Let's stop intellectualizing and start contemplating the truth of what Scripture teaches us in this regard. We will only experience the tremendous blessings which come from actually doing what Psalm 95 tells us to do. We learn to praise and give thanks by doing just that. Then we will find that God truly inhabits the praises of His people.

If genuine praise has gone out of worship, it is because Jesus is no longer the center of our lives. Jesus said, **"And when I am lifted up from the earth, I will draw everyone to myself"**—John 12:32. When we come together to worship God and to offer the sacrifice of love, our hearts should be burning with praise and thanksgiving. If instead our hearts are cold and indifferent, then our actions are an abomination and a lie in God's sight.

"The Lord said: Since this people draws near with words only and honors me with their lips alone, though their hearts are far from me, and their reverence for me has become routine observance of the precepts of men. Therefore, I will again deal with this people in surprising and wondrous fashion: The wisdom of its wise men shall perish and the understanding of its prudent men be hid"—Isaiah 29:13–14.

Our first and foremost duty is to praise and thank God for everything, for He alone is worthy of our praise.

Christian community can only be built on a foundation of sincere praise to our Creator, an acceptance of Jesus as Lord and

Savior, and the indwelling of the Holy Spirit who praises the Father and the Son through us. With Christ at the center of our lives we are truly united to one another in love.

Witness a Christian community at prayer and ask yourself, "Is this a body of believers who are truly in love with their Savior?" If Jesus is truly our beloved Lord and Savior, praise and thanksgiving should flow from the very depths of our beings and be visibly manifest to the world.

How truly sad it is that Christ's followers can feel free to express themselves outwardly with joy for everything except their love of Jesus. We gather in the Lord's house to retell the great message of salvation, to gather in His name, and to remember that our heavenly Father went to great lengths to show His love for us. He sent His Son to suffer and die for us. That's the message we are to recall, and it should bring joy and love to our hearts.

God's first commandment is the most beautiful message because it produces the most magnificent life within us when we act on it. **"Therefore, you shall love the Lord, your God, with all your heart and with all your soul, and with all your strength"**—Deuteronomy 6:5. When we do this, we find that all else falls into place.

Jesus told us to **"seek first the kingdom [of God] and his righteousness, and all these things will be given you besides"**—Matthew 6:33. He also said, **"Come to me, all you who labor and are burdened, and I will give you rest"**—Matthew 11:28.

What cause for joy we have as Christians. So let's open up our hearts and proclaim with our lips our praise and thanks to God, through Jesus, by the power of the Holy Spirit and say, **"With joyful hearts we sing to you our praise and gratitude that you should count us worthy, Lord, to share this heavenly food."**

Take Time To Ponder #6

It's most beneficial if the reflections are written down and pondered often.

- God knows the heart of each person. Have I been too quick to judge someone or his or her situation?
- "Pray as though all depended on God and work as though all depended on me." Do I apply this principle in my life?
- When should I apply the instruction to "pray unceasingly" for a particular intention, and when should I let go and trust, giving thanks for the unknown answer?
- When is my acting in love a hindrance to the growth of another?
- What can I do when a friend constantly depends on me for help but he or she never reaches out to God for help on his or her own?
- Has negativity, discouragement, anger, despair, and loss of faith at any time diminished my life with God?
- What in me or in another person may be blocking or hindering God from answering my prayers?
- As I pray for each intention, are my motives pure? Should I ask God to show me my true motives and ask Him to help me build healthy motives?
- Do I exhibit an attitude of gratitude no matter what circumstance I find myself in? Praising God in all circumstances is the key to joy!
- Do I pray to change God's mind, or do I pray to allow God's grace and His Divine Will to take over my life? Am I willing to exchange my human will for the Divine Will?

Voice Of Love

Inspired text given to author.

I. Remembering
My beloved, how I longed to speak of my love for you;
To reason, to explain, to describe the love and the desire that
Burns and yearns within my Heart for you.
Why have I waited so long to speak, you ask?
Why have I kept my love hidden from you?
What prompts me now to reveal myself?

For now, I will let your questions go unanswered.
For I must first review for you the history of my love.
For in the history you will find answers to many questions you
Haven't even dreamed to ask.

Before I formed you in your mother's womb I knew you and I
loved you.
For it was I who created you.
It was I who desired you from all eternity.
When you came into being in your mother's womb
What joy was in my heart.
For you were so beautiful, so full of potential, so full of
promise.

The world welcomed you into its arms.
It nourished you and cherished you.
Through others I fulfilled your every need and desire.
I brought you to my "house" where you received my life.
You became my child, first created by me,

Now redeemed by me through my son.

What joy and pleasure I took in you
As I watched you grow in your knowledge and love of me.
How I loved your prayers, your efforts
To please me and to respond to my love.
You were my treasure.

II. Questioning

Now my beloved, tell me: why did your love for me cease?
Why did you grow cold and distant?
What came between us?
Perhaps, a reprimand, a misunderstanding, a bad example;
Perhaps, a friend, an incident, a sin; perhaps, fear, insecurity, a
   lie.
Or was it your self-will or your preoccupation with worldly
Things which beckoned you away?
I felt your love die, your zeal cease,
Your attention stray, your goal change.
I reached out time and time again but you moved farther and
   farther
Away from me.

Never have I stopped loving and desiring you.
Never have I closed my heart to you.
Never have I cut you off from all my gifts or abandoned you.
Yet, the more I lavished my gifts on you
The farther you went from my love,
The more independent you became.
I love you, but you have no time to listen to my Word.
I love you, but you have no time or interest in receiving me in
the Eucharist.
I love you, but you are too busy to be bothered with me.

No matter, my beloved.
I will never cease to call you back to me.

For you are mine, and no other love will ever
Satisfy your hungry heart.
I will continually sing my love song to you.

III. Desiring
I beg you; recall the brief moments when you felt my presence.
The moments when your heart leaped for joy and you yearned
for me.
Remember the moments of grace that brought tears to your
eyes ...
Moments when a ray of light shown through to lighten your
heart.

Come to me, yearn for me, desire me as I desire you .Open your
heart, your mind,
Your soul and your spirit to my grace.

Give me your time, your talents, your very life, for they are my
gifts to you.
Only in me will you find the fulfillment you so desire.
Only in me will your heart be at rest.

Speak to me from the depths of your being.
Come; speak to me of the reasons for our broken relationship.
I long to hear you speak.
Come; let us dialogue with one another.

Then, in turn, listen in the depths of your being to My Word.
Receive it in love. Dwell in it and respond to it.
If you open yourself to me you will hear me speak.

Speak, my child, I long to hear your voice.
I long to be united with you once more.
I long to give you once again my priceless Gift, the Bread of
Life.

"Come back to me with all your heart. Don't
let fear keep us apart. Long have I
waited for your coming home to me and
living deeply our new life."*
*Text: based on Hosea. By Gregory Norbert, OSB

Hungry For More?

The late Pope John Paul II publicly stated, "In the dawn of the Third Christian Millennium, the Holy Spirit wishes to enrich Christians with a new and divine holiness" in order to make Christ the heart of the world.

Anyone who is hungry for a more profound and dynamic relationship with Jesus may contact the Center for the Divine Will/ the John Paul II Institute for Christian Spirituality to learn more about this revelation that Jesus shared with Servant of God Luisa Piccarreta (1865–1947). Luisa's cause for beatification is now being reviewed in Rome.

Some of the men and women who seem to have lived in this new and divine holiness include St. Therese of Lisieux; St. Faustina Kowalski; St. Dina Belanger; St. Maximilian Kolbe; St. Hannibal de Francia; Venerable Concepcion Cabrera de Armida; Servant of God Luisa Piccarreta; other religious and laypersons; as well as contemporary Christians who live today in this special relationship.

For more information go online to www.comingofthekingdom. com, or write to the Center of the Divine Will, P.O Box 340, Caryville, TN 37714

Prayer To Release The Holy Spirit

Dear Jesus,

Thank you for the Sacraments of Baptism and Confirmation, when you sent the Holy Spirit to come live within my soul to guide, instruct, and empower me. I ask your forgiveness for not permitting the Spirit to have His way with me in all things. Instead, I seldom thought of Him and almost never asked Him to help me. But now I have come to a better understanding of His role in my life. I no longer want to be a "do-it-myself" Christian.

Therefore, I ask you to release the Spirit's power within me so that I may experience His presence and power in my life. May I now find new meaning in Your Scriptures and in the Sacraments. May I find delight and comfort in prayer and study.

Help me discover the gifts You have bestowed upon me for the good of others and enjoy the peace You promised. I desire to be filled with the Holy Spirit so I can fall passionately in love with You and desire to do only what is pleasing in your sight. And last but not least, help me understand what it means to live in Your Divine Will.

Amen.

CPSIA information can be obtained at www.ICGtesting.com
Printed in the USA
LVOW071952100512

281083LV00001B/4/P

9 781449 743628